1000
OUTSTANDING QUOTES YOU SHOULD KNOW

I0638562

**Compilation and Commentary
By
Lawrence Newman**

1000 Outstanding Quotes You Should Know

Copyright © 2011 by Lawrence Newman

ISBN 978-0-9833921-8-7

Library of Congress Control Number: 2011919803

Printed in the United States of America

Third Edition

Publisher: Silver Millennium Publications, Inc.
           South Elgin, Illinois

TO THE READER

Over the years I took up the habit of collecting quotes that I found inspiring, humorous, informative, and historically enlightening. Many of these quotes are contained within the pages that follow.

I don't always agree with the quotes but didn't feel my own feelings should be the basis for exclusion of a thought provoking statement.

In several cases I've included my own comments about the quote, sometimes based on my understanding that developed over time, and sometimes to give the reader the historical context.

The decision as to how the quotes should be classified was a difficult one. After wrestling with the problem I decided to "mix them up" to allow the reader to have a "kaleidoscope" experience rather than one based on similarity of quotes, or those by the same individual. However, in some cases a couple of quotations were grouped to emphasize a particular subject.

I hope you enjoy this collection of quotes I've selected.

L. Newman
November 1, 2011

1000 OUTSTANDING QUOTES YOU SHOULD KNOW

"Tell a lie often enough and people will believe it's the truth."—Vladimir Lenin, Russian revolutionary and first leader of the Soviet Union, stating a tenet followed by most dictators, including Adolph Hitler, and politicians attempting to destroy the character of their opponents.

"If it bleeds, it leads."—Armstrong Williams, referring to the newspaper, radio and TV adage that bad, even horrific news, will generate more interest and sales than good news.

"We will win because the American people are weak and will not tolerate a long war."—Osama Bin Laden

"Power corrupts, and absolute power corrupts absolutely."—Lord Acton

"We thank God for our homes and our food and our safety in a new land. We thank God for the opportunity to create a new world for freedom and justice."—Elder William Brewster, minister, at the first Pilgrim feast in the New World, considered the first Thanksgiving.

"All men are frightened. The more intelligent, the more they are frightened. The courageous man is a man who forces himself, in spite of his fear, to carry on."—General George Patton

"The only truly dead are those that have been forgotten."—Jewish saying

"I fear we will awaken a sleeping giant and fill him with a terrible resolve."—Japanese Admiral Isuroku Yamamoto, in a diary entry regarding the Japanese plans to attack Pearl Harbor.

"One definition of insanity: Doing the same thing over and over again expecting a different result"—Albert Einstein

"At the end of every diet the path curves towards the trough."—Mason Cooley

"No one appreciates the very special genius of your conversation as a dog does."—Christopher Morley

"Well-behaved women seldom make history."—Bumper sticker

"And so, my fellow Americans, ask not what your country can do for you—ask what you can do for your country."— President John F. Kennedy Inaugural Address. The basic thrust of this thought is traceable back to Cicero.

"Nature, red in tooth and claw."—Alfred Lord Tennyson, alluding to the fact that our observations of nature indicate that, at times, it can be very deadly and bloody as animals struggle to survive by eating the flesh of other animals.

"Many a man in love with a dimple makes the mistake of marrying the whole girl."—Stephen Leacock

"Abandon all hope, ye who enter here!"—From Dante's *Divine Comedy-- The Inferno*

"He and I had an office so tiny that an inch smaller and it would have been adultery."—Dorothy Parker

"You can say any fool thing to a dog, and the dog will give you this look that says, "My God, you're right! I <u>never</u> would have thought of that!"—Dave Barry

"Oh, what a tangled web we weave when first we practice to deceive."—Sir Walter Scott

"Candy is dandy, but liquor is quicker."—Ogden Nash

"Many people will walk in and out of your life but only true friends will leave footprints in your heart."—Unknown

"Diplomacy is the art of saying 'nice doggie' until you can find a rock."—Will Rogers

"The Pope? How many divisions does he have?"—Joseph Stalin, Premier of the Soviet Union, in a response to President Harry Truman at their conference in Potsdam, when Truman told him the Pope was concerned about the future rights of the citizens in the countries being overrun by the Soviet Army.

"Fanaticism consists of redoubling your effort when you have forgotten your aim."—George Santayana

"Let there be spaces in your togetherness."—Kahil Gibran

"We will never save our way to prosperity."—James Schwartz, business owner, making the point that, in the long run, a business cannot insure its long-term profitability just by cutting costs. It must generate sales with good profit margins in order to be successful.

"As for butter versus margarine, I trust cows more than chemists."—Joan Gussow

"There is no 'they', only 'us'."—Bumper sticker

"History will be kind to me for I intend to write it."—Winston Churchill

"Never mistake motion for action."—Ernest Hemingway

"The war situation has developed not necessarily to Japan's advantage."—Taken from an address to the Japanese people by Emperor Hirohito, announcing the country's surrender in World War II, after losing two cities to atom bombs and America's armed forces on Japan's doorstep.

"I fear the Dark Ages may return on the gleaming wings of science."—Winston Churchill

"Don't accept your dog's admiration as conclusive evidence that you are wonderful."—Ann Landers

"A dead cat bounce."—Unknown (refers to the slight gain in a stock market after a huge drop the day before)

"This situation reminds me of a story of a man riding a horse. When one of the horse's rear feet became entangled in one of the stirrups, the man said to the horse, 'If you're going to get on, I'm going to get off'."—President Harry Truman, referring to General MacArthur's interference in foreign policy matters.

"Hard work never killed anybody, but why take a chance?"—Charlie McCarthy

"If you can see the light at the end of the tunnel, you're looking the wrong way."—Barry Commoner

"It has been my experience that folks who have no vices have very few virtues."—President Abraham Lincoln, in response to a criticism of General Grant that he drank too much.

"Find out what brand of whiskey Grant drinks and send a case to each of my other generals."—Attributed to Abraham Lincoln, in his frustration that his other generals never seemed to be on the offensive because they "weren't ready", "unable to locate the enemy" or presumably"outnumbered".

"I am become Death, Shatterer of Worlds."—Robert J. Oppenheimer, leading scientist of the Manhattan project, which developed the atomic bomb, remembering the line from the Indian scripture *Bhagavadgita*, after witnessing the world's first nuclear explosion in the early morning darkness of July 16, 1945 in the desert of New Mexico.

"You are, of course, entitled to your own opinion—but you are not entitled to your own facts."—Unknown

"These ice cubes are seldom used for drinks."—Sign that once hung over the ice cube filled horizontal urinal in the men's room of the Gaslight Restaurant at the O'Hare Hilton Hotel in Chicago.

"The right to be heard does not automatically include the right to be taken seriously."—Senator Hubert Humphrey

"The supreme happiness of life is the conviction that we are loved."—Victor Hugo

"Mozart is sunshine."-Antonin Dvorak, composer of *The New World Symphony*

"Music, the greatest good that mortals know. And all of heaven we have below."—Joseph Addison

"The universe is not hostile, nor yet is it friendly. It is simply indifferent."—John H. Holmes

"Who are we? We find we live on an insignificant planet of a humdrum star, lost in a galaxy tucked away in some forgotten corner of a universe in which there are more galaxies than people."— Carl Sagan

"The fault, dear Brutus, is not in our stars, but in ourselves."— William Shakespeare, from his play "Julius Caesar".

"I am sorry to say that there is too much point to the wisecrack that life is extinct on other planets because their scientists were more advanced than ours."—John F. Kennedy

"If I saw further than others it is because I was standing on the shoulders of giants."—Sir Isaac Newton

"I have never found the companion that was so companionable as solitude."— Henry Thoreau

"I hear and I forget. I see and I remember. I do and I understand."—Chinese proverb

"All great fortunes start with a crime."—Honore de Balzac

"Give a man a fish and you feed him for a day. Teach him to fish and you feed him for a lifetime."—Chinese proverb

"Instead of getting married again, I'm going to find a woman I don't like and give her a house."—Lewis Grizzard

"It is better to keep your mouth closed and let people think you are a fool than to open it and remove all doubt."—Mark Twain

"For three days after death hair and fingernails continue to grow, but phone calls taper off."—Johnny Carson

"Becoming number one is easier than remaining number one."—Bill Bradley, star basketball player and U. S. Senator

"To all the dogs that enriched my life." – Book dedication by Patricia Sherwood for her book "The Quotable Dog Lover".

"The art of writing is the art of discovering what you believe."—Daniel Hare

"Dogs are not our whole life, but they make our lives whole."—Roger Coras

"A single death is a tragedy, a million deaths a statistic."—Joseph Stalin, Soviet Premier, indicating his complete indifference to the many deaths he caused.

"A lie can travel half way around the world before truth gets its boots on."— Mark Twain

"I don't care if it's horse piss. It works."—President John F. Kennedy, responding to a comment from an associate that a laboratory analysis of the injections he was receiving from Dr. Max Jacobson ("Dr. Feelgood") for his back pains, could be dangerous since they contained hormones, steroids, vitamins, enzymes, animal cells and amphetamines.

"Superstition is foolish, childish, primitive and irrational—but how much does it cost you to knock on wood."—Judith Viorst

"Serendipity is looking in a haystack for a needle and discovering the farmer's daughter."—Julius Comroe

"When a man comes to me for advice, I find out what he wants and give it to him."—Josh Billings

"Trouble will rain on those already wet."—Unknown

"Be yourself' is just about the worst advice you can give some people."—Tom Masson

"Few have heard of Fra Luca Parioli, the inventor of double entry bookkeeping, but he has probably had more influence on human life than Dante or Michelangelo."—Herbert Muller

"When two people in business always agree, one of them is unnecessary."—William Wrigley, Jr.

"A decline in courage may be the most striking feature which an outside observer notices in the West today."—Alexander Solzhenitesyn

"Dust thou art and unto dust thou shalt return."—Translation of the Latin words said by the priest putting ashes on the foreheads of Roman Catholics on Ash Wednesday.

"May we live in interesting times."—Drinking toast

"People often say that, in a democracy, decisions are made by a majority of the people. Of course, that is not true. Decisions are made by a majority of those who make them- selves heard and who vote—a very different thing."—Walter H. Judd

"In vino, veritas." (In wine, there is truth)—Pliny the Elder (Be careful what you say "under the influence").

"If you think education is expensive, try ignorance."—Derek Bok

"Use it up, wear it out, make it do or do without."—Unknown

"Who of us is mature enough for offspring before the offspring arrive? The value of marriage is not that adults produce children, but that children produce adults."—Peter deVries

"Tout passe, tout lasse, tout casse." (Everything passes, everything wears out, everything breaks.)—French proverb

"So let me assert my firm belief that the only thing we have to fear is fear itself—nameless, unreasoning, unjustified terror which paralyzes needed efforts to convert retreat into advance."—President Franklin D. Roosevelt, said in the darkest days of the Great Depression.

"History is a race between education and catastrophe."—H. G. Wells

"In two decades I've lost 789 pounds. I should be hanging from a charm bracelet."—Erma Bombeck

"I'll have what she's having."—Diner at nearby table to waiter, after watching Meg Ryan as Sally in *When Harry Met Sally* fake an orgasm.

"Better to reign in hell, than serve in heaven."—Fallen angel Lucifer, from Milton's *Paradise Lost*

"Idle hands are the devil's workshop."—Unknown, quoted when referring to children who have too much free time.

"The 'haves' and the 'have-nots' can usually be traced back to the 'dids' and 'did-nots'."—D. O. Flynn

"Two roads diverged in a wood, and I took the one less traveled by. And that made all the difference."—Robert Frost from his poem "The Road Not Taken".

"If everybody is thinking alike then somebody isn't thinking."—General George Patton

"We love death. The U. S. loves life. That's the big difference between us."—Osama bin Laden, to a reporter, shortly after 9/11.

"You can't go home again."—Author Thomas Wolfe, used in the sense that you can't return to a time of your earlier life and have the same experience—people and places change.

"E pluribus unum" (from many, one)—
Phrase found on all U. S. currency.

"He who defends everything, defends nothing at all."—Frederick the Great, illustrating the tenet that a defender must concentrate his forces.

"Where there's death, there's hope."—University of Illinois Professor Emerson Cammack

"The moving picture is the greatest tool ever devised to shape the mind of man."—Vladimir Lenin, Russian revolutionary leader

"Victory has a hundred fathers but defeat is an orphan."—Galeazzo Ciano

"American society has lost belief in itself. Our artists have become embarrassed to celebrate the extraordinary or the potential for greatness in the nation. And our fears of offending, our pursuit of political correctness, has made our culture bland and timid. This is a road that leads nowhere. It doesn't sustain or give strength, or heighten our collective imagination." —Actor Richard Dreyfuss

"To say my fate is not tied to your fate is like saying 'Your end of the boat is sinking'."—Hugh Downs

"Our long, national nightmare is over. The Constitution works."—President Gerald Ford in an address to the American people after President Nixon had resigned due to the Watergate scandal.

"With malice toward none, with charity for all, with firmness in the right as God gives us to see the right, let us strive on to finish the work we are in, to bind up the nation's wounds, to care for him who shall have borne the battle and for his widow and his orphan, to do all which may achieve and cherish a just and lasting peace among ourselves and with all nations."—Closing words of President Lincoln's Second Inaugural Address, just weeks before the Civil War was to end.

"A frightened captain makes a frightened crew."—Lester Sinclair

"After you begin your first job you can take all your grades and awards you earned during your college years and toss them right out the window. From that point forward the results of your work efforts will determine how successful you will be."—University of Illinois professor Emerson Cammack

"Optimism and pessimism are infectious and they spread more rapidly from the head downward than in any direction. With this clear realization I firmly determined that my mannerisms and speech in public would always reflect the cheerful certainty of victory—that any pessimism and discouragement I might ever feel would be reserved for my pillow."—General Dwight Eisenhower

"Hollywood used to try to entertain Americans, now it tries to indoctrinate them."—Linda Chavez

"What we have here is a failure to communicate." —Prison warden's statement after Luke, the Paul Newman convict character, had been physically disciplined for a rude comment he had made and was lying prostrate on the ground (*Cool Hand Luke*).

"Never send a battalion to take a hill if you have a regiment available."—General Dwight Eisenhower

"Genius is one percent inspiration and ninety-nine percent perspiration."—Thomas Edison

"Is that a gun in your pocket or are you just happy to see me?"—Mae West

"The work assigned will always fill the time allotted."—One of Murphy's Laws

"They take your money and you go home."—From the book *Double Down*, when referring to the conclusion reached regarding Las Vegas casinos by two brothers after gambling away a family fortune.

"Why go out for hamburger when you have steak at home."—Actor Paul Newman when asked what was the reason for the longevity of his marriage to Joanne Woodward.

"Political power grows out of a barrel of a gun."—Mao Tse-Tung

"He is your friend, your partner, your defender, your dog. You are his life, his love, his leader. He will be yours, faithful and true, to the last beat of his heart. You owe it to him to be worthy of such devotion."—Unknown

"Sic semper tyrannus!" (Thus always to tyrants)—Actor John Wilkes Booth, words shouted to the audience after jumping to the stage from the theater box where he had assassinated President Lincoln.

"It's a poor bird that craps in its own nest."—Adele Newman, my mother, an expression she used when referring to some member of a family who disparaged other family members to non-family members.

"General, we're not going for a tie here!"—President George W. Bush, in a teleconference with General George Casey, Commander of American troops in Iraq, after listening to a downbeat assessment of the situation in Iraq, just prior to the president ordering the military surge under the command of General David Petraeus, a major turning point in the war.

"Put a little cold water on your face and get on with your life."—Kathy Boylan, manager of a homeless shelter in Washington, D. C., who shuns air conditioning and asks that others do the same.

"Forgive your enemies, but don't forget their names."—John F. Kennedy

"Retreat, hell! We're just attacking in a different direction!"—Attributed to General O. P. Smith, of the First Marines, in response to a reporter's question asking if the Marines were retreating in North Korea after a massive Chinese attack attempted to encircle them.

"This is not the end; it is not even the beginning of the end, but it may be the end of the beginning."—British Prime Minister Winston Churchill, after British Commonwealth forces had beaten German forces in Northern Africa, during the early days of World War II.

"I saw an angel in the block of marble and I chiseled until I set him free."—Michelangelo

"The most colossal, murderous, mismanaged butchery that has ever taken place on earth."—Writer Ernest Hemingway, bitterly describing the human wave tactics favored by the World War I generals, which consisted of sending lines of soldiers in frontal assaults over open ground strewn with barbed wire emplacements where they were mowed down by machine guns and exploding artillery shells.

"Do you believe in miracles?"—ABC-TV announcer Al Michaels, as the final seconds ticked down in the USA vs. USSR 1980 Winter Olympics semi-final medal round hockey game with the Americans leading 4-3 and the crowd in pandemonium. The American team, composed of collegiate athletes, who went on to win the gold medal against Finland two days later, were given virtually no chance to beat the older and more experienced Soviets who had beaten a team of NHL All Stars a few months earlier.

"Make no little plans; they have no magic to stir men's blood."—Chicago architect Daniel Burnham, describing his underlying philosophy for the planning of the 1893 World's Fair.

"Strange, isn't it? Each man's life touches so many other lives, and when he isn't around he leaves an awful hole to fill, doesn't he?"—Clarence, George Bailey's guardian angel, from the movie *It's A Wonderful Life*, after George had been shown how events would have transpired if George had never been born.

"The next time a sunrise steals your breath away or a meadow of flowers leaves you speechless, remain that way. Say nothing, and listen as heaven whispers, 'Do you like it? I did it just for you."—Max Lucado

"After engaging in the greatest ideological struggle in the history of the world, we won."—William F. Buckley, commenting on the end of the Cold War, when the Soviet Union dissolved and the Russian Communist party was outlawed twenty-one months after the fall of the Berlin Wall.

"The greatest geopolitical catastrophe (of the 20th century)."—Russian president Vladimir Putin, lamenting the demise of the Soviet Union.

"I shall return."—General Douglas MacArthur. Proclaimed in Australia, following his escape from Corregidor, on President Roosevelt's order, as Japanese forces prepared to storm the island. Many in the United States thought he should have said "we" instead of "I", but MacArthur refused to alter his words, leading the phrase to stand as an example of his egotism.

"Peace."—Dr. Robert J. Oppenheimer, leading scientist of the Manhattan Project, which developed the atomic bomb, responding to a question at a Congressional hearing as to what would be a defense to the weapon.

"There is nothing so uncertain as a dead sure thing."—George M. Cohan, commenting on the outcome of sporting events that resulted in spectacular upsets. Examples of this type of upset would be the victory of the US Olympic hockey team of amateurs over the heavily favored Russians in 1980 and the loss of the unbeaten New England Patriots in the 2008 Superbowl.

"I will use treatment to help the sick according to my ability and judgment, but never with a view to injury and wrongdoing."—From the Hippocratic oath of physicians

"Facts are stubborn things; and whatever may be our wishes, our inclinations, or the dictates of our passions, they cannot alter the state of facts and evidence."—John Adams, in defense of the British soldiers in the Boston Massacre trial.

"Some cancer patients recover; some don't. But the ordeal of facing your mortality and feeling your frailty sharpens your perspective about life. You appreciate little things more ferociously. You grasp the mystical power of love. You feel the gravitational pull of faith. And you realize you have received a unique gift—a field of vision others don't have about the power of hope and limits of fear; a firm set of convictions about what really matters and what does not."—Tony Snow, former White House spokesman and news commentator, describing his view of life during his losing battle with cancer.

"The longer I live, the more beautiful life becomes."—Frank Lloyd Wright

"It is a wide road that leads to war and only a narrow path that leads home again."—Russian proverb

"If he does that, he will be the greatest man in the world."—King George III, when told that George Washington would resign his commission and return to private life after leading the American colonies to victory over Great Britain at Yorktown in October 1783. True to his word, Washington resigned his commission only to be recalled from retirement a few years later to serve as America's first president in 1787. Eight years later, after serving two terms as president, he again retired to private life in 1797 and died in 1799.

"They wanted me to be another Washington."—Napoleon Bonaparte, from his deathbed in St. Helena.

"All animals are equal, but some animals are more equal than others." — Restatement of the farm animals' original "commandments" by the pigs after they had consolidated their control of the farm—from George Orwell's *Animal Farm*.

"Four legs good; two legs better."— Another restatement of the farm animals' original commandments, substituting "better" for "bad", after the pigs had learned to walk on their two hind legs-- from George Orwell's *Animal Farm*.

"Faster. Higher. Stronger."—The Olympics motto

"A house divided against itself cannot stand. I believe this government cannot endure permanently half slave and half free."—President Abraham Lincoln

"If I were asked...to what the singular prosperity and growing strength of that people (Americans) ought mainly to be attributed, I should reply: 'To the superiority of their women."—Alexis de Tocqueville, 19th century French political analyst

"The tree of liberty must be refreshed from time to time with the blood of patriots and tyrants."—Thomas Jefferson, an incurable lover of revolution, commenting on an uprising in the American colonies (Shay's Rebellion) shortly after the conclusion of the Revolutionary War.

"We have the wolf by the ears and neither can hold it nor let it go."—Thomas Jefferson, commenting on the institution of slavery in the United States. It would take a civil war, costing over 650,000 casualties, to bring the sad chapter of slavery in the United States to an end.

"I never gave anybody hell. I just told the truth and they thought it was hell."—President Harry Truman, after his successful 1948 "whistle-stop" cam-paign, when people in the crowd would yell out to him on the train's rear platform "Give 'em hell, Harry!".

"In order to enjoy the inestimable benefits that the liberty of the press ensures, it is necessary to submit to the inevitable evils that it creates."— Alexis de Tocqueville, 19th century French political analyst, commenting on press freedom in America.

"Then as now, proximity is power; then as now, proximity is knowledge, and then, as now, proximity helps build loyalty—or at least fear and respect."—Author Jay Winick, from his book, *The Great Upheaval*, commenting on President John Adams's habit of absenting himself from Washington for extended periods, leading inevitably to problems with his cabinet and political maneuvering, undercutting his plans.

"Keep your friends close and your enemies closer."—Vito Corleone, from the movie *The Godfather*

"No one has been barred on account of his race from fighting or dying for America. There are no "white" or "colored" signs on the foxhole or graveyards of America."—President John F. Kennedy, in a message to Congress, presenting his proposed civil rights bill.

"Never eat a meal at a place called 'Mom's' and never play poker with a man named 'Doc'."—Nelson Algren

"When you lay down with dogs, you wake up with fleas."—Benjamin Franklin

"There's no crying in baseball!"—Tom Hanks manager character to one of his weeping team members after she had been criticized, in the movie *A League of Their Own*.

"I do the very best I know how—the very best I can; and I mean to keep doing so until the end. If the end brings me out all right, what is said about me won't amount to anything. If the end brings me out wrong, ten angels swearing I was right would make no difference."—President Abraham Lincoln

"A fanatic is one who can't change his mind, and won't change the subject." – Winston Churchill

"To my critics who say a woman can't think and work and carry a baby at the same time, I'd like to escort that Neanderthal back to the cave."—Alaskan Governor Sarah Palin

"In Germany, they came first for the Communists, and I didn't speak up because I wasn't a Communist. Then they came for the Jews, and I didn't speak up because I wasn't a Jew. Then they came for the trade unionists, and I didn't speak up because I wasn't a trade unionist. Then they came for the Catholics, and I didn't speak up because I was a Protestant. Then they came for me, and by that time no one was left to speak up."—Attributed to Martin Niemoeller

"Yellow cat, black cat, as long as it catches mice."—Deng Xiaoping, Communist Chinese Premier, successor to Mao Tse-Tung, whose pragmatic view on capitalism became the spark that unleashed the entrepreneurial spirit of the Chinese people and catapulted China from a third rate underdeveloped country to a contending superpower in a very short span of years.

"All active mass movements strive to interpose a fact-proof screen between the faithful and the realities of the world. They do this by claiming that the ultimate and absolute truth is already embodied in their doctrine and that there is no truth nor certitude outside it. To rely on the evidence of the senses and reason is heresy and treason."—Eric Hoffer from his book *"The True Believer"*

"There are a thousand hacking at the branches of evil to one striking at the roots."—Henry Thoreau

"Writing is easy. All you do is stare at a blank sheet of paper until drops of blood form on your forehead."—Gene Fowler

I don't aspire to measure the global temperature, nor to estimate the importance of factors which make it. This is not the area of my comparative advantage. But to argue, as it's done by many contemporary environmentalists, that these questions (regarding the negative impact of humans on the environment and our ability to affect it) have already been answered with an unqualified 'yes' and that there is unchallenged scientific consensus about this is unjustified. It is also morally and intellectually deceptive."—Czech President Vaclav Klaus

"Growing old is mandatory; growing up is optional."—Bumper sticker

"The war's over. We've lost."—German Reich Marshall Herman Goering, to an aide, as he left a building in Berlin in 1944 and saw new long-range American P-51 fighters over the city, accompanying American bombers to Germany's capital for the first time.

"(President Clinton) has shown a remarkable disrespect for his office, for the moral dimensions of leadership, for his friends, for his wife, for his precious daughter. It is breathtaking to see the level to which that disrespect has risen."—Senator John Edwards, during the 1999 Senate trial of President Clinton after the President's impeachment for lies arising out of his affair with a White House intern. Nine years later Edwards confessed to an affair with a videographer as he laid the groundwork for his presidential campaign in 2006 and his wife was battling breast cancer.

"Americans can put up with infidelity but hypocrisy is a career ender."—Joanne Ciulla, leadership ethics expert

"To live in hearts we leave behind is not to die."—Thomas Campbell

"The conservative who resists change is as valuable as the radical who proposes it."—Will and Ariel Durant

"Our task now is not to fix the blame for the past, but to fix the course for the future."—President John F. Kennedy

"Any fool can have a child. That doesn't make you a father. It's the courage to raise a child that makes you a father."—Barak Obama, Presidential candidate

"O God, thy sea is so great, and my boat is so small."—Breton fishermen's prayer

"No good deed goes unpunished."—Brooks Thomas

"It's like writing history with lightning. And my only regret is that it is all terribly true."—President Woodrow Wilson, commenting on the landmark film *Birth of a Nation*.

"(There is) an atmosphere of moral mediocrity paralyzing man's noblest impulses. (There is a) tilt of freedom in the direction of evil...evidently born primarily out of humanistic and benevolent concepts according to which there is no evil inherent to human nature."—Alexander Solzhenitesyn

"War is cruelty. There is no use trying to reform it. The crueler it is, the sooner it will be over."—Civil War General William Tecumseh Sherman, stating his views on war from which the phrase "war is hell" was subsequently attributed to him.

"Time eases all things."—Sophocles

"The strong U. S. economy is just on the surface. The backbone is the moral foundation. From the ancient time until now everybody wants to make money. But from history we see only Christians have a continuous creative spirit and spirit for innovation."—Peter Zhao, Communist party member and adviser to the Chinese Central Committee, who converted to Christianity, and has found a growing audience for his message, as Christianity in China has grown from 3 million in the 1970's to at least 54 million today, with some government figures placing it closer to 130 million.

"If you have a hammer, everything looks like a nail."—Bernard Baruch, referring to the inappropriate use of new technology to situations—especially those of a medical nature.

"I went to the woods because I wished to live deliberately, to front only the essential facts of life, and see if I could not learn what it had to teach, and not, when I came to die, discover that I had not lived."—Henry Thoreau

"Yes, I have doubted. I have wandered off the path, but I always return. It is intuitive, an intrinsic, built-in sense of direction. I seem always to find my way home. My faith has wavered but saved me."—Helen Hayes

"I like trees because they seem more resigned to the way they have to live than other things do."—Willa Cather

"It is scarcely the same thing to put a man on the moon as to put a bone in your nose."—William Henry, the late Time Magazine "culture critic" lambasting the current trend of equating the advances of Western civilization with those that emanated from Africa.

"If anyone is crazy enough to want to kill a president of the United States, he can do it. All he must be prepared to do is give his life for the president's."—President John F. Kennedy

"We did not choose to be the guardians of the gate but there is no one else."—President Lyndon Johnson, commenting on the Vietnam war.

"So this is the little lady that made this big war."—President Abraham Lincoln to Harriet Beecher Stowe, upon meeting the author of *Uncle Tom's Cabin*.

"I would rather have this medal than be president of the United States."—President Harry Truman, as he placed the Congressional Medal Of Honor on a World War II medal winner. Anyone who knew the president knew he meant what he said.

"(The answer to that question) is above my pay grade."—Democratic presidential nominee Barak Obama, in response to a question as to when human life begins, at the Saddleback Forum in 2008.

"Only your real friends will tell you when your face is dirty."—Sicilian Proverb

"I would rather live my life as if there is a God and die to find out there isn't , than live my life as if there isn't and die to find out there is."—Albert Camus

"In the process of thinking throughout that day in November, each person was drawn to a thought, even more personal than the memory of the President. In seeing that respected man, who had everything, pass from life in a single unsuspecting instant, there was the thought of each person's own mortality—their own straight lines that began with birth, that would end with death, and the length between so unknown. The President, who was able to have so much under control, was not master of the length of that line. And perhaps his message to the world was exactly that. For everyone in the world received that message—no matter what language they spoke, no matter what God they worshiped."—Taken from the film narrative of *Years of Lightning, Day of Drums,* highlighting President Kennedy's accomplishments and death.

"The winds and the waves are always on the side of the ablest navigators."—Edward Gibbon

"Most of us have far more courage than we ever dreamed we possessed."—Dale Carnegie

"Often do the spirits of great events stride on before the events, and in today already walks tomorrow."—Samuel Taylor Coleridge

"The graveyards are full of indispensable men."—Charles DeGalle

"Leadership is the capacity to translate vision into reality."—Warren G. Bennis

"If you have a job without aggravation, you don't have a job."—Malcolm Forbes

"I have made this letter longer because I lack the time to make it shorter."—Blaise Pascal, illustrating the point that a well-composed letter requires time.

"You are remembered for the rules you break."—General Douglas MacArthur

"Well, I don't know as I want a lawyer to tell me what I cannot do. I hire him to tell me how to do what I want to do."—J. P. Morgan

"Never doubt that a small group of committed citizens can change the world. Indeed, it is the only thing that ever has."—Margaret Mead

"After the game the king and the pawn go into the same box."—Italian proverb

"Either we are alone in the universe, or we are not. Either thought is frightening."—Arthur C. Clarke

"The true test of independent judgment is being able to dislike someone who admires us."—Sydney J. Harris

"I have lived to thank God that all my prayers have not been answered."—Jean Ingelow

"When the president does it, that means it is not illegal."—Richard Nixon, to David Frost, in an interview several years after his resignation from the U. S. presidency.

"It would indeed be a tragedy if the history of the human race proved to be nothing more than the story of an ape playing with a box of matches on a petrol dump."—David Ormsby Gore

"I keep six honest serving men. (They taught me all I know.) Their names are What and Why and When and How and Where and Who."—Rudyard Kipling

"If time travel is possible, then where are the tourists from the future?"—Stephen Hawking

"Self respect is the root of discipline. The sense of dignity grows with the ability to say no to oneself."—Abraham Heschel

"Their attitude toward us might resemble our own attitude toward an ant hill. Our inclination is not to bend down and offer the ants beads and trinkets, but simply to ignore them."—Michio Kaku, commenting on the probable attitude of extraterrestrial life towards earth. From his book *Physics of the Impossible*.

"We have only to kick in the door and whole rotten structure will come crashing down."—Adolf Hitler to General Alfred Jodl, during the early phases of the German invasion of the USSR in June 1941.

"God himself could not sink this ship."—response of a member of Titanic's crew to a passenger inquiring whether the ship was really unsinkable.

"Let them eat grass."—Andrew Myrick, after cutting off credit to hungry Sioux Indians on the Redwood Agency in Minnesota in early April 1862. During the uprising by the Sioux later that month, Myrick was killed, and his mouth found stuffed with grass.

"Whether you like it or not, history is on our side. We will bury you."—Premier of the Soviet Union, Nikita Khrushchev, to a group of Western diplomats

"If we gave refunds for bad weather days we'd have to charge twice as much for good weather days."—Sign in sailboat chartering office

"In a war of ideas it is people who get killed."—Stanislaw J. Lec

"That's not going to last."—Comic George Lopez's doctor's "compass-ionate" response to the comic's answer of "good", when the doctor initially asked how he felt after being diagnosed with advanced kidney disease.

"I had a rose named after me and I was very flattered. But I was not pleased to read the description in the catalog—'Not good in bed but fine against the wall'."—Eleanor Roosevelt, wife of President Franklin D. Roosevelt

"Rotting garbage, manure and stinky socks."—Some of the descriptions given by most people encountering the odor of a durian, the world's smelliest fruit, loved by Chinese and Southeast Asians, and considered a delicacy by them.

"I can't spare him. He fights."—President Lincoln when Congress and even Mary Lincoln, his wife, called for General Grant's head after the terrible carnage in May and June 1864, when the Union forces suffered some 52,000 casualties in about six weeks, a figure approaching the number of men killed in the entire Vietnam War. At Cold Harbor alone, 9,000 men were lost in one hour.

"Mars has global warming but without a greenhouse and without the participation of Martians."—Dr. Habibullo Abdusamatov, head of the Space Research Laboratory at St. Petersburg's Pulkovo Astronomical Observatory, a strong believer that it is the sun's cyclical changes in its irradiance which control the earth's temperature, pointing out that the polar ice caps on Mars have been shrinking, in parallel with global warming on earth. From Lawrence Solomon's book *The Deniers*.

"Congress will push me to raise taxes, and I'll say 'no'. And they'll push again and I'll say to them, 'Read my lips. No new taxes'."—Republican candidate for President, George H. W. Bush, to tremendous cheers and applause at their convention in August 1988. Contrary to his pledge he agreed to raise taxes in 1990. He lost his reelection bid to Bill Clinton in 1992.

"If slaves will make good soldiers our whole theory of slavery is wrong."—Confederate General Howell Cobb, an ardent slave holder, arguing against the enlistment of slaves in the Confederate army in early 1864 as the war turned against the South. Later that year, when Union General William Tecumseh Sherman came across Cobb's plantation during his historic march through Georgia he instructed his men to "spare nothing". Every building on Cobb's plantation was burned to the ground except the slave quarters.

"You don't want the truth. Because deep down, in places you don't talk about at parties, you want me on that wall. You want me there. We use words like honor, code, loyalty. We use these words as the backbone to a life defending something. You use 'em as a punchline. I have neither the time nor the inclination to explain myself to a man who rises and sleeps under the blanket of the very freedom I provide, then questions the manner in which I provide it."—Jack Nicolson as Marine Colonel Nathan Jessup to officer questioning him during a court of inquiry into the death of a Marine. (From the movie *A Few Good Men*).

"If it tastes good, spit it out."—The Cardiologist's Diet, Unknown

"Your proctologist called--he found your head."—Bumper sticker

"Thanks to the interstate highway system, it is now possible to travel from coast to coast without seeing anything."—Charles Kuralt

"I like not only to be loved, but to be told I am loved; the realm of silence is large enough beyond the grave."—George Eliot

"Rum, sodomy and the lash."—Winston Churchill, sarcastically listing British naval traditions, as he saw them, when told that his policies, as First Lord of the Admiralty, were detrimental to the traditions of the British navy.

"There is something terrible yet soothing about returning to a place where you once lived. You are one of your own memories."—Mary Morris

"You find out life's this game of inches, and so is football. Because in either game, life or football, the margin for error is so small. I mean, one half a step too late or too early, and you don't quite make it."—Al Pacino, as his character head coach Tony D'Amato, talking to his football team before they took the field. (From the movie *Any Given Sunday*).

"Your mother's flesh sticks in my teeth."—a common insult uttered by the inhabitants of Easter Island in the Pacific, as their sources of food severely diminished due to overcrowding, and they turned to cannibalism. As related by Jared Diamond in his book *Collapse*.

"If the stars should appear just one night in a thousand years, how would men believe and adore!"—Ralph Waldo Emerson

"It can be cold. You can get lonely. You can be hurt and sore. These are just challenges. There are challenges every day. Any woods can beat you no matter how good of a woodsman you are. I haven't lost my respect and awe for what God has placed out there for me to see and appreciate. Never." — M. J. "Eb" Eberhart, age 70, 1,400 miles and 46 days into his effort to hike the 4,400 mile North Country Trail, as related to Rick Olivo of *The Daily Press*, Ashland, Wisconsin.

"It's the people, the places, the pain
  and the trials,
 It's the joy and the blessings that come
  with the miles.
 It's the calling that's gone out to a
  fortunate few,
To wander the fringes of God's hazy
  blue.—M. J. "Eb" Eberhart

"A dog wags its tail with its heart."—
Martin Buxbaum

"Accept and embrace and enjoy suffering."—Mental training philosophy of the Gym Jones boot camp.

"Hope is a thing with feathers, that perches in the soul, and sings the tune without the words, and never stops at all."—Emily Dickinson

"The loons were calling, I can hear them yet, echoes rolling back from the shores and from unknown lakes across the ridges until the dusk seemed alive with their music."—Sigurd Olson. To hear the wail of the loon during a quiet evening on a Northern lake is an experience that pierces you to your soul—a sound never to be forgotten.

"There has never been an age that did not applaud the past and lament the present."—Lillian Eshler Watson

"He used the World Almanac and just went down the list by population (after) Washington gave (General) Lemay the green light. His bombers burned 64 more cities (after his incendiary attack on Tokyo by 346 B-29 bombers gutted 16 square miles of the city on March 9, 1945).

* * *

"In the strange calculus of war LeMay helped prevent an estimated one million American casualties and upwards of two million Japanese by helping push Japan's Emperor Hirohito to surrender before the invasion (by American troops, scheduled for November 1945).

* * *

"Today, some question whether the ends justified the means. In 1945, no American with a husband, brother or son serving in the military did. For them, the speediest end of that horrible conflict was the only goal."—Warren Kozak, author of *LeMay: The Life and Wars of General Curtis LeMay.*

"If a man does not keep pace with his companions, perhaps it is because he hears a different drummer. Let him step to the music he hears, however measured or far away."—Henry Thoreau

"The eyes are the window of the soul."—Ancient proverb

"No nation can sustain its values by claiming to support the soldier while opposing the mission. The truth is that the nation determines the mission."—Bing West

"I can with truth assure you, that I heard the bullets whistle. Believe me, there was something charming in the sound."—Major George Washington, age 22, in a letter describing his first military encounter with the enemy, during the French and Indian War (May 1754).

"If I had my life to live over, instead of wishing away nine months of pregnancy, I'd have cherished every moment and realized that the wonderment growing inside of me was the only chance in life to assist God in a miracle...I would have sat on the lawn and not worried about grass stains...When my kids kissed me impetuously I would never have said, 'Later. Now go get washed up for dinner."—Erma Bombeck

"In the factory we make cosmetics; in the store we sell hope."—Charles Revson

"When they are five years old they have all the questions. When they are seventeen they have all the answers."—Unknown

"A life without love is like a year without summer."—Swedish proverb

"There are no true friends in politics. We are sharks circling and waiting, for traces of blood to appear in the water."—Alan Clark

"We give dogs time we can spare, space we can spare. And in return, dogs give us their all. It's the best deal man has <u>ever</u> made."—M. Acklam

"If there are no dogs in heaven, then when I die I want to go where they went."—Will Rogers

"Better to have him inside the tent pissing out, than outside the tent pissing in."—President Lyndon Johnson, of J. Edgar Hoover, head of the FBI.

"Several excuses are always less convincing than one."—Aldous Huxley

"I made up a ticket for his gasoline and made him sign it, but I wouldn't let him pay for it. I just wanted to be able to say that I treated President Harry S. Truman to a tank of gasoline."—Gas station owner Carroll Kehne.   Ex-president Harry Truman and his wife, Bess, had stopped at his station in Frederick, Maryland, June 21, 1953, on their solo cross-country car trip from Independence, Missouri to Washington, D. C., some six months after Truman left office.   Their round-trip 2500-mile journey, was made on roads existing before the interstate highway system was built, without any escort of Secret Service agents. This incident is related in Matthew Algeo's book, *Harry Truman's Excellent Adventure—The True Story of a Great American Road Trip*.

"It depends on what the meaning of 'is' is."—President Bill Clinton, answering a question via videotape for a grand jury, as a result of his affair with a White House intern.

"The link between the burning of fossil fuels and global warming is a myth. It is time the world's leaders, their scientific advisers and many environmental pressure groups woke up to the fact"

* * *

"...carbon dioxide is *not* the dreaded killer greenhouse gas...It is, in fact, the most important airborne fertilizer in the world... (vital for photosynthesis).

* * *

"The real truth is that the main greenhouse gas—the one that has the most direct effect on land temperatures—is water vapour, 99% of which is entirely natural."—Excerpts from a full page article titled "Global Warming? What a Load of Poppycock!" in the London newspaper, *The Daily Mail*, by Professor David Bellamy, an ardent environmentalist.

"An invasion of armies can be resisted, but not an idea whose time has come."— Victor Hugo

"You don't marry one person; you marry three: the person you think they are, the person they are, and the person they are going to become as a result of being married to you."—Richard Needham

"Plain women know more about men than beautiful women do."—Katherine Hepburn

"Science cannot answer the deepest questions. As soon as you ask why there is something instead of nothing, you have gone beyond science. I find it quite improbable that such order came out of chaos. There has to be some organizing principle. God to me is the explanation for the miracle of existence—why there is something instead of nothing."—Cosmologist Allan R. Savage

"Anyone who isn't confused doesn't really understand the situation."—Edward R. Murrow, on the Vietnam War.

"Say not that you know a man entirely till you have divided an inheritance with him."—Johann Kaspar Lavater

"Ocian in view! O! the joy."—Entry in the journal of William Clark, November 7, 1805, as he, Meriwether Lewis and their party completed their 1-½ year expedition through the northern portion of the unmapped wilderness of the Louisiana Purchase, which began in St. Louis, enduring near starvation and hostile Indians along the way. His spelling may have been bad but the outpouring of emotion he felt at seeing the Pacific Ocean off the coast of Oregon can be felt.

"You can't get rid of poverty by giving people money."—P. J. O'Rourke

"Oh, to be only half as wonderful as my child thought I was when he was small, and half as stupid as my teenager now thinks I am."—Rebecca Richards

"Security is mostly a superstition. It does not exist in nature, nor do the children of men as a whole experience it. Avoiding danger is no safer in the long run than outright exposure. Life is either a daring adventure or nothing."—Helen Keller

"Now he belongs to the ages."—Edwin Stanton, Secretary of War, as President Lincoln expired early in the morning of April 16, 1865, as a result of the bullet wound to his head he received the previous evening at Ford's Theater.

"Having a young child explain something exciting he has seen is the finest example of communication you will ever see or hear."—Bob Talbert

"Love doesn't make the world go round. Love is what makes the ride worthwhile."—Franklin P. Jones

"Love: to feel with one's whole self the existence of another being."—Simone Weil

"Without music, life is a journey through a desert."—Pat Conboy

"Advice is what we ask for when we already know the answer but wish we didn't."—Erica Mann Yong

"Liberté! Égalité! Fraternité! (Liberty! Equality! Fraternity!)—motto of the French Revolution

"Here on earth usually when you're trapped in something, what's good is on the outside. In a spacecraft, what's good is on the inside and what's outside is death."—Astronaut Frank Borman

"The concept of two people living together for 25 years without a serious dispute suggests a lack of spirit only to be admired in sheep."—A. P. Herbert

"One of the best ways to measure people is to watch the way they behave when something free is offered."—Ann Landers

"The most difficult thing in the world is to know how to do something and to watch someone else doing it wrong without comment."—Theodore White

"We now know that the extra carbon dioxide and global warmth, no matter what their cause, are resulting in a gradual greening of the Earth. There is some evidence that there has been a slight poleward shift in the habitats of some warm weather species, from the tropics where there is a great diversity of life, to higher latitudes where many of these forms of life could not otherwise survive. Global warming has made weather less severe, and cold weather is known to cause more deaths than hot weather. So why is global warming necessarily a bad thing?"—Roy W. Spencer, from his book *Climate Confusion*.

"The nice part about being a pessimist is that you a constantly being either proven right or pleasantly surprised."—George F. Will

"Kill them all! God will recognize his own."—Arnold-Arnay, abbot of Cite-aux, when asked how the true Catholics could be distinguished from the heretics at the Massacre of Beziers, 1209. This quote morphed into an updated version in the 20th century, when soldiers encountered situations where enemy combatants were mixed in with civilian populations. The quote then became, "Kill them all and let God sort them out."

"You know you've read a good book when you turn the last page and feel a little as if you have lost a friend."—Paul Sweeney

"I walked by the Union Square Bar. I was going to go in. Then I saw myself— the reflection in the window—and I thought, 'I wonder who that bum is.' And then I saw it was me. Now look at me. I'm a bum. Look at me. Look at you. You're a bum. Look at you. And look at us. Look at us. C'mon, look at us. See? A couple of bums."—Jack Lemmon, as his character, Joe Clay, an alcoholic, speaking to his wife, played by Lee Remick, also an alcoholic. (From the motion picture *Wine and Roses*)

"There can be no other occupation like gardening in which, if you creep behind someone at their work, you would find them smiling."—Mirabel Osler

"Being president is like being a jackass in a hailstorm. There's nothing to do but to stand there and take it."—President Lyndon Johnson

"Like being a rat in the jaws of a giant terrier."—Apollo 8 astronaut Bill Anders, describing the shaking experienced by an astronaut during a blastoff on top of a Saturn rocket, which developed the thrust of 540 jet fighters, as it consumed ten thousand pounds of fuel a second and created a thunderous, earth trembling roar only second in intensity to an atom bomb blast.

"A fellow asked me that once and I said I don't know, but I do know people who know how much they are worth generally aren't worth very much."— Bunker Hunt's response to Congressman Jim Rosenthal's question asking how much he was worth, at a Congressional Committee inquiry in May 1980, held to investigate the Hunt brothers attempt to corner the silver market.

"However long the night, the dawn will break."—African proverb

"It is easy to go down into Hell...; but to climb back again, to retrace one's steps to the upper air—there's the rub..."—Virgil

"Perhaps it would be a good idea, fantastic as it sounds, to muffle every telephone, stop every motor and halt all activity for one hour someday just to give people a chance to ponder for a few minutes on what it's all about, why they are living and what they really want."—James Truslow Adams

"More than any other time in history, mankind faces a crossroads. One path leads to despair and utter hopelessness –the other, to total extinction. Let us pray we have the wisdom to choose correctly."—Woody Allen

"You want to run out in front, prepare to be tripped from behind."—S. A. Sachs

"Wait till Foxx sees <u>me</u> hit."—Ted Williams, cocky 20 year old Boston Red Sox rookie, to teammate who had told him, "Wait till you see (Hall of Famer Jimmie) Foxx hit." Williams went on to become, many believe, the greatest hitter in baseball and the last player to hit over .400 in a season (.406 in 1941). His career accomplishments seem even more astonishing considering the fact that he spent nearly five years flying Marine Corps fighter planes in World War II and the Korean War during his prime years.

"Not only did we play the race card, we played it from the bottom of the deck."— Robert Shapiro, on the defense's conduct during the O. J. Simpson trial.

"There is no such thing on earth as an uninteresting subject; the only thing that can exist is an uninterested person."— G. K. Chesterton

"As a human being, one has been endowed with just enough intelligence to be able to see clearly how utterly inadequate that intelligence is when confronted by what exists."—Albert Einstein

"Did you ever think that making a speech on economics is a lot like pissing down your leg? It seems hot to you but is never does to anybody else."—President Lyndon Johnson

"Make yourself happy today. Mind your own business."—Ann Landers

"The art of cross-examination is not the art of examining crossly. It's the art of leading the witness through a line of propositions he agrees to until he's forced to agree to the *one final question*."—Clifford Mortimer

"The legislative process is a little bit like sausage making and the sausage factory is not an attractive place."—David Axelrod, one of President Obama's top advisors, commenting on the declining support for the president's healthcare plan during the contentious con-gressional debate.

"Money, not morality, is the principal commerce of civilized nations."—Thomas Jefferson

"Train yourself to use your hands and fingers . . . Keep your knives sharp. Above all, have a good time."—Julia Child, commenting on her philosophy of cooking.

"The broad mass of a nation will more easily fall victim to a big lie than to a small one."—Adolf Hitler

"I believe that this nation should commit itself to achieving the goal, before the decade is out, of landing a man on the moon and returning him safely to earth."—President John F. Kennedy, May 25, 1961

"Mr. President, the *Eagle* has landed."—note left at the gravesite of President Kennedy in Arlington National Cemetery, July 20, 1969—the day Neil Armstrong set foot on the moon.

"Here men from the planet Earth first set foot on the moon. July 1969 A. D. We came in peace for all mankind."—Plaque left on the moon by the American astronauts.

"Who today is willing to say that Texas and California and the remainder of the Southwest would be better off if it were ruled by Mexico?"—Stephen Ambrose

"The essence of life is statistical improbability on a colossal scale."—Richard Dawkins, from his book *The Blind Watchmaker*

"The side that stays within its fortifications is beaten."—Napoleon, a maxim of war which was ignored with devastating effect by his own country's generals prior to World War II when they built the supposedly impregnable Maginot Line to defend France against any future assault by German armies. The Germans simply went around it.

"The best guarantee of (worker) efficiency is a long line (of job seekers) at the factory gate."—Samuel Insull

"The most important ally Great Britain has, next to America, is Corporal Schiklgruber and his strategic brilliance."—Prime Minister Winston Churchill, during World War II, referring to Adolf Hitler, using the German dictator's World War I rank and his original family name on his father's side. Hitler's strategic blunders included invading the Soviet Union and declaring war on the United States. The film of Hitler's war declaration shows the jaws of many of the generals in the audience dropping open in disbelief.

"It appears the president is going to double-down tonight and try to put lipstick on this pig and call it something else."—Rep. John Boehner, referring to President Obama's forthcoming speech on proposed healthcare legislation.

"I have seen very good colonels become very bad generals."—Maurice de Saxe

"I tremble for my country when I reflect that God is just; that his justice cannot sleep forever."—Thomas Jefferson, referring to the slavery issue.

"No civilization is complete which does not include the dumb and defenseless of God's creatures within the sphere of charity and mercy."—Queen Victoria

"There are two kinds of atheism: one tends to dispense with the idea of God, and the other to deny His intervention in human affairs."—Joseph Joubert

"Just think! Some night the stars will gleam upon a cold, grey stone, and trace a name with silver beam. And lo! T'will be your own."—opening lines from a poem by Robert William Service.

"An army of deer led by a lion is more to be feared than an army of lions led by a deer."—Chabrias, Greek general

"Sometimes it seems like that is the choice—either kick ass or kiss ass."—James Caan

"Our waking hours form the text of our lives; our dreams the commentary."—Unknown

"If you smell fish, run like hell!'—pithy warning to the technicians and engineers involved with fueling the Army Redstone rocket used to send America's first satellite into orbit in early 1958. Its fuel was a derivative of nerve gas, one drop of which was fatal to humans.

"Don't complain. The people who will listen can't do anything about it, while the people who can do something about it won't listen."—John Hebert

"If I stop one heart from breaking, I shall not live in vain."—Emily Dickinson, from her poem *Not In Vain.*

"Oh, hear us when we cry to Thee, for those in peril on the sea!"—excerpt from the Navy Hymn, *Eternal Father, Strong to Save.*

"He who plants a tree, plants a hope."—Lucy Larcom, from her poem *Plant A Tree.*

"The only way to get rid of a bad law is to enforce it vigorously."—President U. S. Grant. This philosophy was followed by the "wets" seeking to overturn Prohibition in the early 1930's as they put forth measures to substantially increase law enforcement budgets to go after alcohol drinkers These proposals were constantly voted down by the "drys".

"Your friend is the man who knows all about you, and still likes you."—Elbert Hubbard

"That's all the bullets we had."—Sheriff Grady Judd, Polk County, Florida, to media inquiries as to why a fugitive hiding in a wooded area had been shot 68 times by a SWAT team. The man had executed a deputy, who had stopped his car, shooting him eight times, including a shot behind his right ear at close range.

"I fired (Gen. Douglas MacArthur) because he wouldn't respect the authority of the President. I didn't fire him because he was a dumb son-of-a-bitch, although he was, but that's not against the law for generals. If it was, half to three quarters of them would be in jail."—Harry S. Truman

"No, you can't."—final words of President John F. Kennedy, in response to Nellie Connelly, wife of Senator John Connelly, when she said, "You sure can't say Dallas doesn't love you, Mr. President.", as they rode in their motorcade, moments before the President was assassinated.

"International conferences: Social functions at which statesmen who know something is wrong agree that nothing can be done about it."—Leo Rosten

"My flesh will turn to ash and clay. But I'll be here—somehow—some way."—Don Blanding, from his poem *Somehow*.

"A lawyer with his briefcase can steal more than a hundred men with guns."—Don Corleone, from the movie *The Godfather*.

"The cowards never started—and the weak died along the way."—Unknown settler, who made the trek across the Oregon Trail (1845).

"The woods are lovely, dark and deep. But I have promises to keep. And miles to go before I sleep. And miles to go before I sleep."—Robert Frost, from his poem *Stopping by Woods on a Snowy Evening*.

"If the Third World War is fought with nuclear weapons the fourth will be fought with bows and arrows."—Lord Louis Mountbatten

"Comrades! The cult of the individual acquired such monstrous size chiefly because Stalin himself, using all conceivable methods, supported the glorification of his own person."—Nikita Khrushchev, in a closed session of the 20th Congress of the Communist Party.

"We speak words, we hear meanings."—Unknown

"We are drowning in information, but starved for knowledge."—John Naisbitt

"Have three men do five jobs and pay them like four."—Arnold Donald

"Cow 1 is not Cow 2 is not Cow 3. . . ."—S. I. Hayakawa, from his outstanding book on semantics, *Language in Thought and Action*, conveying the thought that the characteristics of one element in a group does not mean that all others in the group have the same attributes; everyone and everything is different to some degree. It is the characteristics of an individual member that must be defined, not those assumed because one is a member of a certain group.

"Do not place military cemeteries where they can be seen by replacements marching to the front."—General George Patton, in advice to his commanders.

"A basic rule of organization is to build the fewest possible management levels and forge the shortest possible chain of command.—Peter Drucker

"I still remember the refrain of one of the most popular barrack ballads of that day (around the turn of the century) which proclaimed most proudly that 'Old soldiers never die, they just fade away.' And like the old soldier of that ballad, I now close my military career and just fade away—an old soldier that tried to do his duty as God gave him the light to see that duty. Goodbye."—General Douglas MacArthur, closing his speech before a joint session of Congress, shortly after President Harry Truman had relieved him of his command in Korea.

"A managerial job is defined by relationships—upwards, downwards and sideways."—Peter Drucker

"I paint things as I think of them, not as I see them."—Pablo Picasso

"Be sincere. Be brief. Be seated."—Franklin D. Roosevelt, giving advice on speechmaking.

"As every combat veteran knows, war is primarily sheer boredom punctuated by moments of stark terror."—Colonel Harry Summers

"Figuring out who you are is the whole point of human experience."—Anna Quindlen

"The most miraculous thing is happening. . . .The physicists are getting down to the nitty-gritty; they've just about pared things down to the ultimate details, and the last thing they ever expected to happen is happening. God is showing through. They hate it, but they can't do anything about it. Facts are facts.—John Updike

"Are we never to learn that socialism has its roots in envy and in nothing else."—Norman Douglas

"Security is the basic issue in Afghanistan. Whatever it takes we should do it. History will judge us harshly if we allow the hope of a liberated Afghanistan to evaporate because we failed to stay the course."—Senator Joe Biden, 2002. Seven years later, as vice president and advisor to the president, his "stay the course" warning morphed into a "cut and run" recommendation, in which surgical air strikes from offshore would replace boots on the ground, a strategy which would almost certainly lose the war, provide a haven for Muslim terrorists, destabilize a nuclear armed Pakistan and destroy America's credibility throughout the world.

"I think that I shall never see, a poem as lovely as a tree. . . . Poems are made by fools like me. But only God can make a tree."—Joyce Kilmer, from his poem *Trees*, killed on the Western Front, July 30, 1918.

"One of the worst things that can happen in life is to win a bet on a horse at an early age."—Danny McGoorty

"The most important sex organ is the brain."—Unknown

"We share the air with the forests and the water with the seas. As a body they and we are one."—Buddha

"A garden grows people as well as plants."—Unknown

"After I am dead I would rather people wonder why I do not have a monument than why I do have one."—Cato The Elder

"As we acquire more knowledge, things do not become more comprehensible, but more mysterious."—Albert Schweitzer

"Nothing changes more consistently than the past; for the past that influences our lives does not consist of what actually happened, but of what men believe happened."—Gerald W. Johnson

"The greatest sign of success for a teacher is to be able to say, 'The children are now working as if I did not exist'."—Maria Montessori, founder of Montessori schools.

"There's nothing sadder in this world than to awake Christmas morning and not be a child."—Erma Bombeck

"No snowflake in an avalanche ever feels responsible."—Voltaire

"It is vain to be done with more what can be done with fewer."—William of Occam (1349). This principle became known as "Occam's Razor", which states that in attempting to explain some problem or event it is the simplest explanation that is probably the most accurate.

"I say this a lot, and I probably shouldn't: the difference between rape and seduction is salesmanship."—Bill Carpenter, mayor of Independence, Missouri. You're right—you shouldn't say it. Stupid.

"A wise man's question contains half the answer."—Ibn Gabriol

"Quarrels would not last long if all the fault was on one side."—Duc de la Rochefoulcauld

"We do not see things as they are. We see them as we are."—The Talmud

"If it's working, keep doing it. If it's not working, stop doing it. If you don't know what to do, don't do anything."—Medical School advice to prospective doctors.

"Every problem was once a solution to a previous problem."—Bob Mandel

"All the laws in the world won't stop a man with a gun."—Detective Mike Stone, from the TV series "The Streets of San Francisco". Or anyone with a knife or a bomb.

"If you hold a cat by the tail you learn things you cannot learn any other way."—Mark Twain

"There are two things that are more difficult than making an after-dinner speech: climbing a wall which is leaning toward you and kissing a girl who is leaning away from you."—Winston Churchill

"We are all visitors to this time, this place. We are just passing through. Our purpose here is to observe, to learn, to grow, to love, and then we return home."—Australian Aboriginal saying

"We are what we eat."—Adele Davis

"We can't all be heroes. Some of us have to stand on the curb and clap as they go by."—Will Rogers

"The lady with all the answers does not have the answer to this one."—Ann Landers, on her divorce.

"It's a strange paradox for a great wordsmith, but whenever Obama makes an important policy speech these days he leaves everyone totally confused. I have come to the conclusion that the real reason this gifted communicator has become so bad at communicating is that he doesn't really believe a word that he is saying."—Tina Brown, *Daily Beast* blogger.

"The creation of a thousand forests is in one acorn."—Ralph Waldo Emerson

"If you've never been hated by your child, you have never been a parent."—Bette Davis

"The one who loves the least controls the relationship."—Dr. Robert Anthony

"I don't think I can live without you, but make just half the bed and I'll try."—Note to husband from his wife, after she found only his half of the bed was made.

"It is not the strongest of the species that survive, nor the most intelligent, but the one most responsive to change."—Charles Darwin

"When I lay my head on the pillow at night and I can say I was a decent person today.   That's when I feel beautiful."—Drew Barrymoore

"I'm not a role model... Just because I dunk a basketball doesn't mean I should raise your kids."—Charles Barkley

"Love without conversation is impossible."—Mortimer Adler

"The most exciting phrase to hear in science, the one that heralds new discoveries, is not 'Eureka!' but 'That's funny...'."—Issac Asimov

"Democracy is two wolves and a lamb deciding what to have for lunch."—Benjamin Franklin

"There's no doubt that today's players are far superior athletes and leapers. But now it's an individual sport. Back then we played together as a team. That's why we may have beaten them."—Detroit Mayor Dave Bing, selected as one of the best 50 NBA players of all time, commenting on today's NBA players.

"Send me food or send me bullets."—Telegram sent to Washington by General Douglas MacArthur, commander of the occupation forces in Japan, following their World War II surrender, after the U. S. government had refused his initial request for food to feed the starving Japanese.

"It's for you."—Actor A. E. Mathew to a fellow actor during a stage play after forgetting his lines as he picked up a ringing phone.

"Unprepared, half-asleep catatonics who drift in late and leave early."—Jackson Toby, in his book *The Lowering of Higher Education in America*, describing many of today's crop of college undergrads who can't write with minimal competence or understand basic cultural references.

"I am not a crook!"—President Richard Nixon, during the time of the Watergate investigation.

"I am not a whore!"—Rachel Uchitel, one of the many admitted extramarital liaisons of golf star Tiger Woods, during an interview.

"The lady doth protest too much, methinks."—from the play *Hamlet* by William Shakespeare.

"I wish I'd stayed home."--Epitaph in a ghost town graveyard, after the gold rush.

"When I stand on the open prairie early in the morning, just as dawn is breaking, I feel closer to God than anywhere else in the world."—From a rancher's diary. One can also experience this feeling seeing the first rays of the sun break the horizon from a boat or from the shore of a lake or ocean.

"Someone's hair should be on fire."—Democratic Rep. Jane Harmon, referring to the lack of action by U. S. officials after a Nigerian terrorist's father warned the U. S. embassy that his son had been radicalized. The terrorist subsequently boarded a U.S. bound plane and almost succeeded in blowing it up as it prepared to land in Detroit.

"Life is good whether it is long or short. I feel like going into the wild is a calling all feel, some answer and some die for."—Final texted words of Bryce Gillies as he lay dying, found on his Blackberry. Gillies, an experienced hiker, celebrating his 20th birthday, had gone solo hiking on a back country trail in the Grand Canyon during July 2009, took a wrong turn and later died from dehydration and sunstroke, after he found himself on a precipice 80 feet high, a half mile from the Colorado River, without the strength to return the tortuous way he had come. Gillies was one of 12 people who died in the Grand Canyon in 2009. (From a story in *The Arizona Republic* by Richard Ruelas).

"A light-skinned African-American with no Negro dialect—unless he wanted to have one."—Democrat Senate Majority leader Harry Reid characterizing Barack Obama, during Obama's efforts to secure the Democratic presidential nomination.

"Mountains are the beginning and the end of all natural scenery."—John Ruskin

"2030—then we take over."—T shirt worn by some Islamic residents in Stockholm, Sweden. From the book *While Europe Slept* by Bruce Bawer, a critique of the open immigration policies of Europe that has allowed a significant influx of Muslims into Europe, who refuse to integrate into the communities or accept Western values, and whose birth rates far exceed those of the country's other citizens. The author points out that the Muslim immigrants have taken over much of Malmo, Sweden, which has become a "no-go" area to others.

"Ridiculous. Black history is American history."—Morgan Freeman, actor, on being asked what he thought of Black History Month.

"He chose to lead some of the toughest missions over Germany. This man was, and is, a hero and leader in every sense of the word. God, how we need one like him at the helm today."—John H. Peterson, former captain in a B-26 bomber group, in a letter to the editor of *The Wall Street Journal*, describing Colonel James Stewart, who led 25 missions over Germany during World War II, after enlisting in the Army as a private. Stewart had an outstanding film career including a Best Actor Academy Award in 1941.

"These proceedings are closed."—General Douglas MacArthur, at the end of the Japanese surrender signing ceremony on the battleship Missouri in Tokyo Bay, September 2, 1945. At this point, as planned, 400 B-29s and 1,500 carrier aircraft, flew over the massed fleet of 257 Allied ships—1,364 days since the attack on Pearl Harbor.

"No other nation in the world teaches a national history that leaves its children feeling negative about their own country—this would be the first."—Albert Shanker of the American Federation of Teachers, denouncing the draft of history standards, a government financed study, proposed by a group of left-leaning educators. The United States Senate censured the standards 99-1, which were later revised to eliminate the leftist slant that pervaded the original document.

"Alexander the Great, Julius Caesar and all the other great generals of history failed in the end, because of their occupation policies. I will not make that mistake."—General Douglas MacArthur, to his aide as they toured the bombed out ruins of Tokyo, following Japan's surrender. His benevolent postwar policies in Japan are considered one of the most enduring and praiseworthy monuments of his career. To this day he is revered by the Japanese.

"A closed mind is a dying mind."—Edna Ferber

"The best things you can give your children, next to good habits, are good memories."—Sydney J. Harris

"Whoever said, 'It's not whether you win or lose that counts,' probably lost."—Martina Navritilova

"Food banks are struggling and American children depend on school nutrition programs for survival, while audiences view eating contests as entertainment. And that's more obscene than any X-rated movie will ever be, in my opinion."—From a Dear Abby column.

"I remember how my father used to raise a glass each evening at the dinner table—a glass of the finest tap water. Looking at his eight children, he'd say, 'Water: best drink on the planet'."— Judith Freeman, raised as a Mormon, who later relaxed her view on alcohol and sipped cocktails and wine, but still considers water her favorite drink.

"Football combines the worst features of American life. It is violence punctuated by committee meetings."—George Will

"Time is a great teacher. Unfortunately it kills all its pupils."—Hector Berlioz

"What don't you understand about the word 'illegal'?"—Question asked of those supporting the rights of illegal immigrants in the United States.

"C'mon, this guy would have been serving us coffee a couple of years ago."—Ex-president Bill Clinton to Senator Ted Kennedy, characterizing Barack Obama, in an attempt to solicit Kennedy's endorsement of Bill's wife, Hillary, for the Democratic nomination for president.

"Children are the living messages we send to a time we will not see."—John H. Whitehead

"You can make more friends in a month by being interested in them than in ten years by trying to get them interested in you."—Charles L. Allen

"When you have to make a choice and don't make it, that is in itself a choice."— William James

"Those who are blessed with the most talent don't necessarily outperform everyone else. It's the people with follow-through who excel."—Mary Kay Ash

"I've always thought that America stands for (rewarding success). You finish high school. You work hard, go to college and hope you succeed in life. I never knew it was a class war—that those who succeed in life are the ones that have to bear all the burden."—Chicago Mayor Richard M. Daley, criticizing the recent stiff tax hikes on those earning $125,000 or more voted in by Oregon voters—and an indirect criticism of the Obama administration's plan to do the same with the federal tax.

"For anyone who is alone, without God and without a master, the weight of days is dreadful."—Albert Camus

"I feel lousy about the pain that I've caused my wife and kids. I feel guilty and conscience-stricken, and all of those things you think sentimental, but which my generation calls simple human decency. And I miss my home, because I'm beginning to get scared shitless, because all of a sudden it's closer to the end than the beginning, and death is suddenly a perceptible thing to me, with definable features."—William Holden as Max Schumacher, to his girlfriend, from the movie *Network*.

"They got together and made a pact with the devil."—Pat Robertson, evangelist, attributing the 2010 Haiti earthquake to God's punishment for the Haitian people's supposed pact with the devil during the time they were fighting for their independence from France in the early 1800's. This statement is equaled only in its stupidity with that of the actor Danny Glover who attributed the earthquake to global warming.

"Love is like war: easy to begin but very hard to stop."—H. L. Mencken

"Luck is what happens when preparation meets opportunity."—Seneca

"Most problems precisely defined are already partially solved."—Harry Lorayne

"Faith moves mountains, but you have to keep pushing while you are praying."—Mason Cooley

"Tell me who you're with and I'll tell you who you are."—Spanish proverb

"What have you done today to help reach your lifelong goals?"—Brian Tracy

"The important thing in the Olympic Games is not winning but taking part."—Pierre de Coubertin, founder of the modern Olympic Games, expressing an ideal not always followed by the participants, or the countries they represent.

"I did not wish to take a cabin passage, but rather to go before the mast and on the deck of the world, for there I could best see the moonlight amid the mountains."—Henry David Thoreau

"Nobody ever went broke under-estimating the taste of the American public."—H. L. Mencken

"Kissing - and I mean like, yummy, smacking kissing - is the most delicious, most beautiful and passionate thing that two people can do."—Drew Barrymore

"Between tomorrow's dream and yesterday's regret is today's opportunity."—Unknown

"We make a living by what we get, but we make a life by what we give."—Sir Winston Churchill

"The best inheritance a parent can give his children is a few minutes of his time each day."—O. A. Battista

"Excuses are the nails to build a house of failure."—Don Wilder

"ARBEIT MACHT FREI" (Work sets you free)—Infamous sign over the entrance to the largest extermination camp for Jews, in Auschwitz, Poland, during World War II. Ash flakes from the large, tall chimneys of the crematoriums, continually fell from the sky onto the camp 24 hours around the clock.

"Experience is a hard teacher because she gives the test first, the lesson afterwards."—Vernon Law

"If you want my final opinion on the mystery of life and all that, I can give it to you in a nutshell. The universe is like a safe to which there is a combination. But the combination is locked up in the safe."—Peter De Vries

"I am a part of everything that I have read."—Theodore Roosevelt

"We must hate—hate is the basis of Communism. Children must learn to hate their parents if they are not Communists."—Vladimir Lenin

"Man is the only animal that can remain on friendly terms with the victims he intends to eat until he eats them."—Samuel Butler

"Without Spam we wouldn't have been able to feed our army."—Russian Premier Nikita Khrushchev, commenting on the Hormel canned pork product that became a staple of the American, British and Russian armed forces during World War II.

"Parents need to fill a child's bucket of self-esteem so high that the rest of the world can't poke enough holes in it to drain it dry."—Alvin Price

"You may have to live on coconuts. In that case, live on coconuts."—portion of Japanese Army directive to Lt. Hiro Onodo, who was directed to lead combat patrols against enemy forces on the Philippine island of Lubang. After losing all his command to desertion or death Lt. Onodo surrendered to Philippine forces on March 7, 1974, twenty-nine years after World War II ended.

"Character contributes to beauty. It fortifies a woman as her youth fades. A mode of conduct, a standard of courage, discipline, fortitude and integrity can do a great deal to make a woman beautiful."—Jacqueline Bisset. And these words seem just as applicable to improving a man's appearance.

"Decision is a sharp knife that cuts clean and straight. Indecision is a dull one that hacks and tears and leaves jagged edges behind."—Jan McKeithen

"Cause change and lead; accept change and survive; resist change and die."—Ray Norda

"If it doesn't fit, you must acquit"—Johnny Cochran, lead defense lawyer for O. J. Simpson, summing up a murder case to the jury, pointing out that the glove worn by the murderer of Simpson's wife and Ronald Goldman apparently did not fit Simpson, after the prosecution blundered and asked Simpson to put on the blood stained shrunken glove.

"Being taken for granted can be a compliment. It means that you've become a comfortable, trusted element in another person's life."—Joyce Brothers

"I tended to faint when I saw accident victims in the emergency ward, during surgery, or while drawing blood."—Michael Crichton, prolific writer of best selling novels, including *Jurassic Park*, originally trained as a physician.

"It's not easy to cut through a human head with a hacksaw."—Michael Crichton

"Every normal man must be tempted, at times, to spit on his hands, hoist the black flag, and begin slitting throats."—H. L. Mencken. A strong statement, but one that could have relevance when one thinks of the vengeful thoughts by many Americans following that fateful day in September 2001 when almost 3000 innocent lives were snuffed out.

"No good movie is too long, and no bad movie is too short."—Roger Ebert

"A hundred times a day I remind myself that my inner and outer life depends on the labors of other men, living and dead, and that I must exert myself in order to give in the same measure as I have received and am still receiving."—Albert Einstein

"No car with my name on it is going to have a Jap engine in it."—Henry Ford II, Ford Motor Company, turning down the offer of Honda, a small Japanese automaker, to furnish four cylinder engines during the mid-1970s. After its offer was scorned Honda took the more risky path of building car manufacturing plants for cars bearing its name in the United States. The long decline of the American auto industry can be dated from this point.

"Speakers who talk about what life has taught them never fail to keep the attention of their listeners."—Dale Carnegie

"The greatest danger for most men lies not in setting our aim too high and falling short, but in setting our aim too low and achieving our mark."—Michelangelo

"The belief that there are other life forms in the universe is a matter of faith. There is not a single shred of evidence for any other life forms, and in forty years of searching, none has been discovered. There is absolutely no evidentiary reason to maintain this belief."—Michael Crichton

"Global warming is necessary to prevent a new Ice Age."—Conclusion of an article in *Science* magazine (January 2010).

"Only the broken-hearted know the truth about love."—Mason Cooley

"The great cause which divides our countries is not to be decided by individual animosities."—Thomas Jefferson to British Brig. General William Phillips, who was being held captive in Virginia during the Revolutionary War. Jefferson insured that Phillips and other officers were ensconced in mansions close to Jefferson's Monticello home and Jefferson was invited to lavish dinners at his captive's mansion, which were attended to by slaves assigned to the captive general. After being released in a prisoner exchange the general, using the intelligence he gathered while a prisoner, returned leading a military force, targeting Virginia and Jefferson himself, who had to make a timely escape to avoid capture. From *Flight From Monticello* by Michael Kranish. I guess we could say that Jefferson was just a bit naïve.

"Friends are sometimes boring, but enemies never."—Mason Cooley

"If you seek (Alexander) Hamilton's monument, look around. You are living in it. We honor Jefferson, but live in Hamilton's country—a mighty industrial nation with a strong central government."—George Will

"God gives every bird his worm but He does not throw it into the nest."—Swedish proverb

"The most important thing in communication is to hear what isn't being said."—Peter Drucker.

"In three words I can sum up everything I've learned about life: It goes on."—Robert Frost

"I made my money by selling too soon."—Bernard Baruch

"There's no such thing as work-life balance. There are work-life choices, and you make them and they have consequences."—Jack Welch, CEO, General Electric

"If you're reading this document, it means I'm no longer with you."—Opening line of document prepared by Bea Toney Bailey, which lays out her future wishes upon her death. Included with the document is an obituary notice she prepared. She suggests everyone prepare their own obituary as a favor to their family at a time when they are grieving.

"In love, we worry more about the meaning of silences than the meaning of words."—Mason Cooley

"What if the system collapses? Everybody is looking to me, and I don't have the answer. I am really scared."—Secretary of the Treasury Henry Paulson to his wife, in mid-September, 2008, prior to the bankruptcy of Lehman Brothers which threatened to bring down the entire U. S. financial system. From his book *On The Brink*.

"We know the truth, not only by reason, but also by the heart."—Blaise Pascal

"It used to be *civilized*. The media was on our side. We'd get our work done by one o'clock and by two we were at the White House chasing women. We got the job done and the reporters focused on the issues . . . It was *civilized*."—Senator Ted Kennedy to Andrew Young, aide to Senator John Edwards, recalling the way things were in the early 60s. From Young's book *The Politician*, an exposé of the political self destruction of Senator Edwards.

"Washington's character was rock solid. He came to stand for the new nation and its republican virtues, which was why he became our first President by unanimous choice."—Stephen Ambrose. Contrast this quote with the previous one when seeking a definition of character.

"There is no hunting like the hunting of man, and those who have hunted armed men long enough and liked it, never care for anything else thereafter."—Ernest Hemingway

"Ask yourself whether the dream of heaven and greatness should be waiting for us in our graves—or whether it should be ours here and now and on this earth."—Ayn Rand

"You'll be going to sleep, and when you wake up, Mommy will be right here. I love you. Now give me a kiss."— Recommended words for mothers to tell their young children before they enter surgery—from a Dear Abby column, in response to a request from an operating room nurse who said she is sometimes faced with hysterical crying mothers who have to peeled off their children.

"And any time I see a Paris Hilton story or an American Idol audition, I admire him even more."—Mitch Albom, *Tribune Media Service*, commenting on J. D. Salinger, author of *Catcher In The Rye*, a best-selling rite-of-passage book for teenagers, who died at age 91. Salinger had moved to a 90 acre spread in New Hampshire back in the 1960s after he wrote his best seller, cutting off all outside contact. "Salinger wanted people to clap for the right things—his stories, not his private life, his interviews, or the movie version of his work. I admired him for that."

"I would suggest that the projections might be a bit optimistic."—Karl Compton, Letters to the Editor in *The Wall Street Journal*, when he pointed out that the plans for the construction of a $40 billion dollar bullet train system from Los Angeles to San Francisco is projecting 41 million riders per year (40% of breakeven). " . . . that works out to 112,328 riders per day or 4680 per hour. With 150 passengers packed cheek-to-jowl into each car, that's a 31-car train leaving every hour of the day and night." Since a round-trip air ticket goes for approximately $200, one has to question how many travelers would want to pony up the $400 for a one-way train ticket. Anyone else have a multibillion-dollar boondoggle idea to build a terrorist target in an earthquake prone region?

"Chains do not hold a marriage together. It is threads, hundreds of tiny threads which sew people together through the years."—Simone Signoret

"(Hurricane Katrina) was the best thing that happened to the education system in New Orleans."Secretary Of Education Arne Duncan, a statement for which he later apologized. However, the underlying truthfulness of the statement was borne out by the substantial increase in school test scores and the improvement of the school system to the point that Louisiana became a leading contender for Race To The Top education grants set aside for model school systems. Prior to the hurricane there had been 24 indictments of school employees and $91 million in federal education funds unaccounted for.

"People don't care what they look like in public because they don't care about the public. . . It seems that the richer this country gets, the more slovenly people have become. It's a grim scene . . ."— Froma Harrop, *Providence Journal*, from her column titled "America: A Nation of Slobs".

"(I'm disappointed that the Supreme Court did not) break free from the essential constraints that were placed by the founding fathers in the Constitution."—President Barack Obama in his 2010 State of the Union address, criticizing the Court, for a recent decision, whose members were sitting nearby. If the constraints are essential why would they break free from them?

"This president is a real slow learner."—Mayor Oscar Goodman of Las Vegas, responding to the latest gaffe of President Obama who told a New Hampshire crowd "not to blow a bunch of cash on Vegas". A year earlier the president had cautioned companies receiving a federal bailout not to hold their corporate meetings in Las Vegas, which caused numerous cancellations of corporate events and contributed to a 13% unemployment rate in the area. Mayor Goodman had recently changed his party affiliation from Democrat to Independent.

"The young man knows the rules, but the old man knows the exceptions."—Oliver Wendell Holmes Sr.

"Sometimes the best, and only effective, way to kill an idea is to put it into practice."—Sydney J. Harris

"Harassed by a thousand details, all of them unimportant, he was too weak-willed to arrive at a reasonable and fruitful arrangement of his time."—Thomas Mann, from his novel *Buddenbrooks*, set in the 1870s, describing its main character, the executive Thomas Buddenbrooks. One has to wonder how Buddenbrooks would have fared in today's business environment of emails, voice mail and web-surfing.

"We were kidnapped and brought here against our will from Africa. We didn't land on Plymouth Rock—the rock landed on us."—Malcolm X

"You don't have to be old in America to say of a world you lived in: That world is gone."—Peggy Noonan

"He who would learn to command well must first of all learn to obey."—Greek saying

"Everyone has an invisible sign hanging from their neck saying, 'Make me feel important'. Never forget this message when working with people."—Mary Kay Ash

"When guns are outlawed, only outlaws will have guns."—Unknown

"You can conquer almost any fear if you will only make up your mind to do it. For remember, it doesn't exist anywhere but in the mind."—Dale Carnegie

"I still find each day too short for all the thoughts I want to think, all the walks I want to take, all the books I want to read, and all the friends I want to see."—John Burroughs

"Leave God out of it. Men make war, not God."—Response from an elderly man to a woman who had said, "If there was a God He would have shown some mercy to them.", after the devastating bomb attack on Hamburg, Germany, during World War II as she watched bodies being stacked into trucks. From *The American Heritage Picture History of World War II*.

"Day is done/Gone the sun/From the lakes/From the hills/From the sky/All is well/Safely rest/God is nigh."—Taps.

"I find that the curiossity of our party is pretty well satisfyed with rispect to this anamal."—A tongue-in-cheek comment from the journal, of Merriwether Lewis, replete with misspellings, describing the feelings of his men after the initial encounters the Lewis and Clark expedition of 1804-06 had with grizzly bears. The men, who had discounted the tales about the animal from the Indians, were amazed at the ferocity of the huge beast even after it had been shot several times. After their first few meetings, during which some of the men barely escaped with their lives, they tended to avoid them.

"To avoid criticism, do nothing, say nothing, be nothing."—Elbert Hubbard

"There is no merit in putting off a war for a year if, when it comes, it is far worse or much harder to win."—Winston Churchill

"What lawsuit? What kind of person would do that? My son is dead and that wouldn't bring him back."—David Kumaritashvili, of the country Georgia, responding angrily to the question as to whether the family would sue to hold officials responsible for the death of their son, Nodar, during a practice luge run in Vancouver, Canada, prior to the Winter Olympics in February 2010. Contrast this view to that of most Americans in today's obscenely litigious society, whose mantra is: "Sue me. Sue you. Sue everybody." Life is full of risks, many of which are your choice. Take responsibility for these choices and don't look for somebody to blame when things turn out badly.

"Lack of outdoor time has been linked not only to increased obesity, but depression, stress, diabetes, ADD, and poor performance in the classroom. It's time parents took advantage of an old-fashioned remedy to our children's obesity program. Let's fling open the back door and let kids do what comes naturally, running around in green spaces and making friends with nature."—Kevin Coyle, *National Wildlife Federation*.

"The next time he gives a speech, someone should tap him on the ankle and say, 'Mr. President, we're down here.'".—Charles Blow, *New York Times* columnist, chiding Obama for not speaking "in the plain words of plain folks."

"Here rests in honored glory an American soldier known but to God."—Inscription on the Tomb of the Unknown Soldier.

"I'd rather be a real good one-term president than a mediocre two-term president."—President Barack Obama in an interview with Diane Sawyer. One would normally expect a "real good" president to be reelected.

"If you give me six lines written by the hand of the most honest of men, I will find something in them which will hang him."—Cardinal Richelieu, 18th century France

"Once the mujahedeen conquer Afghanistan we'll aim for the Middle East and Europe."—al Queda bomb maker, from the *Frontline* film "Behind Taliban Lines", expressing their goal to kill all "unbelievers".

"Remember, democracy never lasts long. It soon wastes, exhausts and murders itself. There never was a democracy yet that did not commit suicide."—President John Adams

"We may be likened to two scorpions in a bottle, each capable of killing each other, but only at the risk of his own life."—J. Robert Oppenheimer, leading scientist on the Manhattan Project that developed the atomic bomb, describing the situation of the United States and the Soviet Union, shortly after the Soviet Union acquired atomic weapons.

"No man is an island, entire of itself;...any man's death diminishes me, because I am involved in mankind, and therefore never send to know for whom the bell tolls; it tolls for thee."—John Donne

"And when the last scene of all comes, and death takes the master in its embrace, and his body is laid away in the cold ground, no matter if all other friends pursue their way, there by his graveside will the noble dog be found, his head between his paws, his eyes sad but open in alert watchfulness, faithful and true even in death."—George Graham Vest, closing line from his *Eulogy on a Dog* speech during a lawsuit. A court observer said, "I looked at the jury and saw all were in tears."

"Show me the manner in which a nation or a community cares for its dead. I will measure exactly the sympathies of its people, their respect for the laws of the land, and their loyalty to high ideals."—William E. Gladstone

"I wish to have no connection with any ship that does not sail fast; for I intend to go in harm's way."—John Paul Jones

"A democracy cannot exist as a permanent form of government. It can only exist until the voters discover that they can vote themselves largesse from the public treasury. From that moment on the majority always votes for the candidates promising the most benefits from the public treasury with the result that a democracy always collapses over loose fiscal policy, always followed by a dictatorship. The average age of the world's greatest civilizations has been 200 years."—Alexander F. Tytler. Let's all hope he's wrong.

"Today is the first day of the rest of your life."—Charles Dederich

"There is no true intimacy between souls who do not know how to respect one another's solitude."—Thomas Merton

"If there is one single secret to long life, that secret is moderation."—George Gallup

"I may not know much, but I know chicken shit from chicken salad."—Senator Lyndon Johnson, commenting on a speech by Richard Nixon.

"There is no reason for any individual to have a computer in their home."--Ken Olson, President of Digital Equipment Corporation, 1977

"No pleasure is worth giving up for two more years in a geriatric home."--Kingsley Amis

"The lion and the calf shall lie down together, but the calf won't get much sleep."—Woody Allen

"King Heroin is my Shepard, I shall always want. He maketh me to lie down in the gutters. He leadeth me beside the troubled waters. He destroyth my soul. He leadeth me in the paths of wickedness for the effort's sake. Yea, I shall walk through the valley of poverty and will fear all evil for thou, Heroin, art with me. The needle and capsule try to comfort me. Thou strippest the table of groceries in the presence of my family. Thou robbest my head of reason. My cup of sorrow runneth over. Surely heroin addiction shall stalk me all the days of my life and I will dwell in the House of the Damned forever."— Unknown. "The Psalm of the Addict." This quote should be read by all those in favor of drug legalization and those considering the use of hard drugs.

"Those who make peaceful revolution impossible will make violent revolution inevitable."—President John F. Kennedy

"Love is the magician, the enchanter that changes worthless things to joy, and makes right royal kings and queens of common clay. It is the perfume of that wondrous flower, the heart, and without that sacred passion, that divine swoon, we are less than beasts; but with it, earth is heaven, and we are gods."—Robert G. Ingersoll

"There is a land of the living and a land of the dead and the bridge is love, the only survival, the only meaning."— Thornton Wilder, final sentence from *The Bridge of San Luis Rey*.

"It reminds me of the Army thesis that it two half-wits are assigned to a task, you get a whole wit, whereas the mathematical prospect is, more accurately, that what comes out will be a quarter-wit."—Brig. General S. L. A. Marshall, commenting on the decisions of various "egghead" committees held during the Vietnam War.

"Gentlemen do not read each other's mail."—Secretary of State Henry L. Stimson, upon closing his department's code-breaking office in 1929. Luckily, the War Department, had no such gentlemanly compunctions and years later was successful in breaking the Japanese codes, which contributed to the epic American victory at Midway in June 1942.

"People will soon get tired of staring at a plywood box every night."—Darryl Zanuck, President of 20th Century Fox, deriding television as a fad.

"Your *people*, sir, is nothing but a great beast!"—Alexander Hamilton to Thomas Jefferson

"Dogs are like mirrors. Their behavior is a reflection on the owner's ability to give and receive love."—Michell Frankenberg

"Now it is not men's figure skating—no, it is dancing."—Russian figure skater Evgeni Plushenko, after winning the silver medal at the 2010 Winter Olympics, suggesting publicly he was robbed since he performed skating's hardest jump during his performance—the quadruple toe loop, something the gold medal winner did not perform.

"If you want to jump, go do track, field or pole vault. This is not the circus."—Octavio Cinquanta, president of the International Skating Union, which established a new Olympics skating scoring system, reacting to Russian figure skater Evgeni Plushenko's comments, after Plushenko did not win the gold medal.

"Let me not mourn for the men who died fighting, but rather let me be glad that such heroes have lived."—General George Patton

"As Einstein showed, the closer an object gets to the speed of light, the faster it moves through time. Traveling at 99% of the speed of light for 2.8 years (a spaceship) would take you over 17 years into the future (on earth). Time travel is hard work. . . To get a 100-ton spaceship to 99% of the speed of light would take the output of all American power stations running for around 3,700 years."—Brian Clegg

"That's an amazing invention, but who would ever want to use one of them?"—President Rutherford B. Hayes, after participating in a telephone conversation between Philadelphia and Washington.

"The most astounding fact about reformers, driven by the purest of motives and most spotless goodwill, is that it does not dawn on them that their programs can make things worse."—Leo Rosten

"I shake my head, terrorized by the idea of being circumcised in a sheepfold, amidst fleas and mice, with an old rusty knife."—Italian Journalist Daniele Mastrogiacomo, captured by the Afghanistan Taliban, after seeing the head of his driver severed with a knife, and told by his captors that he would be spared if he converted to Islam. He was considering the conversion until told he would have to be circumcised. Eventually the Italian government convinced the Afghan government to exchange some Taliban prisoners for the Italian journalist. From Mastrogiacomo's book *Days of Fear*.

"If I had known, I would have become a watchmaker."—Albert Einstein, whose theories led to the development of the atomic bomb.

"Immature love says, 'I love you because I need you.' Mature love says I need you because I love you.'"—Erich Fromm

"In Italy for thirty years under the Borgias they had warfare, terror, murder, bloodshed—they produced Michelangelo, Leonardo da Vinci and the Renaissance. In Switzerland they had brotherly love, five hundred years of democracy and peace and what did that produce. . . ? The cuckoo clock." — Orson Welles's character, Harry Lime, from the movie *The Third Man*.

"Love me a little less, but longer."—Folk saying

"We do not quite forgive a giver. The hand that feeds us is in some danger of being bitten."—Ralph Waldo Emerson

"Until the day of his death no man can be sure of his courage."—Jean Anouilh

"We therefore commit his body to the ground; earth to earth, ashes to ashes, dust to dust."—Book of Common Prayer

"Give us the child for eight years and it will be a Bolshevik forever."—Vladimir Lenin

"Audace, audace, toujours audace. (Audacity, audacity, always audacity)."—Motto on plaque outside US Army Command and General Staff College, Leavenworth, Kansas.

"Long live Stalin! Long live the proletarian revolution!"—Shouts by those about to be executed after being convicted during the Stalin instituted purge trials of the 1930s.

"Some people think broadcasting into the universe is like shouting in a jungle—not necessarily a good idea."—Seth Shostak, senior astronomer at the SETI Institute, commenting on the concern of some astronomers that purposefully sending messages into outer space seeking to make contact with aliens could attract those who aren't necessarily benign.

"There are few things more painful than to recognize one's faults in others."—John Wells

"If Jesus were alive he would be an account executive in an advertising agency."—Bruce Barton, from his book *The Man Nobody Knows*. Rather strange premise for a book since most people think Jesus would probably be working with his hands, like perhaps—a carpenter.

"Democracy is sand driven by the wind."—Benito Mussolini

"Don't worry, major. You never hear the one that gets you."—Colonel Douglas MacArthur to Major George Patton, when Patton flinched as an enemy shell landed close by in World War I.

"Under the Einstein formula ($E=mc^2$) a single gram of matter, four-tenths the weight of a dime, would lift a million-ton load to the crest of a mountain six miles high."—William Manchester, from his book *The Power and the Glory*.

"When the gods want to punish us, they grant our prayers."—Danish Proverb

"Those who love you, make you cry."—Italian proverb

"The estimated number of stars in the universe is equal to all the grains of sand on all the beaches on earth."—Robert Ciconne, astrophysist.

"The seed of everything that has happened in the Universe was planted in that first instant; every star, every planet and every living creature in the Universe came into being as a result of events that were set in motion in the moment of the cosmic explosion...The Universe flashed into being, and we cannot find out what caused that to happen."—Astrophysicist Robert Jastrow, describing the moment of creation known as the Big Bang—14 billion years ago.

"I look at the universe and I know there's an architect."—Jack Anderson

"There are times when silence has the loudest voice."—Leroy Brownlow

"My father gave me the greatest gift anyone can give another person—he believed in me."—Jim Valvano

"By recording your dreams and goals on paper, you set in motion the process of becoming the person you most want to be."—Mark Victor Hansen

"Self delusion is pulling in your stomach when you step on the scales."—Paul Sweeney

"A married couple that plays cards together is just a fight that hasn't started yet."—George Burns

"Sex is hardly ever just about sex."—Shirley McClaine

"A generation which ignores history has no past and no future."—Robert Heinlein

"Death is not extinguishing the light; it is putting out the lamp because dawn has come."—Rabindranath Tagore

"To get rich is glorious."—China Premier Deng Xiaoping, 1984, whose policies began the transformation of Communist China from a backward third-rate country into an economic powerhouse of the 21st century.

"It was involuntary. They sunk my boat."—John F. Kennedy, on being asked how he became a war hero.

"Annual income twenty pounds, annual expenditure nineteen pounds, result happiness. Annual income twenty pounds, annual expenditure twenty pounds, ought and six, result misery."—Mr. Micawber from *David Copperfield* by Charles Dickens. Perhaps there's a lesson here for local, state and federal governments.

"Do you remember in classical times when Cicero had finished speaking, the people said, 'How well he spoke', but when Demosthenes had finished speaking they said, 'Let us march'."—Adali Stevenson, introducing John F. Kennedy to the 1960 Democratic convention, after they had nominated Kennedy as their presidential candidate.

"Imagination without skill gives us modern art."—Tom Stoppard

"When I was a boy of 14, my father was so ignorant I could hardly stand to have him around. But when I got to be 21 I was astonished at how much the old man had learned in seven years."—Mark Twain

"We can search for villains on ideological grounds, but it's a waste of time. Compromise and flexibility are necessary in politics. Purity in martyrdom is for suicide bombers."—Indiana Governor Mitch Daniels

"From the smallest necessity to the highest religious abstraction, from the wheel to the skyscraper, everything we are and everything we have comes from one attribute of man—the function of his reasoning mind."—Ayn Rand

"Politicians will always spend every penny of tax raised and whatever else they can get away with."—Economist Milton Friedman

"It was a lot of work, because when you have the word 'ever' in a question about baseball it means going back to 1876, which is when Major League Baseball began . . . the year of Custer's Last Stand."—Steve Hirdt, of Elias Sports Bureau, official statistician for major league sports, regarding a question whether the home run hit by San Diego Padres outfielder Jody Gerut, the first man up to bat in the first game played in a brand-new stadium, Citi Field, new home of the New York Mets, was the first time that had happened. It was.

"There's sand in the porridge and sand in the bed, and if this is pleasure we'd rather be dead."—Noel Coward, in a short limerick describing his beachfront vacation.

"We have a whole generation of people thinking it's OK to approach bears. In shark country if you holler "shark" everyone gets out of the water. In the bear world, if you holler "bear" everybody runs into the woods."—Chuck Bartlebaugh of the Be Bear Aware campaign, shortly after a fatal bear attack near Yellowstone National Park. (As reported in the *Missoulian*)

". . . a document that was later called the longest suicide note in history."—Martin Rubin, describing the 1983 manifesto of Britain's Labor Party that advocated, among other things, unilateral nuclear disarmament and nationalization of the country's industries. This document was cited as the principal reason for the two landslide victories of the Conservative Party's Margaret Thatcher.

"You shall not press down upon the brow of labor this crown of thorns, you shall not crucify mankind upon a cross of gold."—William Jennings Bryan, famed orator and 1896 presidential candidate, in the concluding words of his famous "Cross of Gold" acceptance speech to the Democratic convention, railing against the backing of U. S. currency by gold, which many saw as restricting the country's money supply resulting in the economic depression of the time. Immediately after uttering the above words, Bryan stepped back and threw his arms out to his sides in a Christ-like pose. After a few seconds of silence the convention audience exploded into a tumultuous roar that went on for several minutes.

"This is no time for making new enemies."—Voltaire, on his deathbed, on being asked to renounce the devil.

"The chief business of the American people is business."—President Calvin Coolidge

"Our ships have been salvaged and are retiring at high speed toward the Japanese fleet."—World War II Admiral Bill Halsey's radio message to U. S. naval headquarters after Japanese claims that most of the U. S. Third Fleet had either been sunk or retired.

"An intellectual is somebody who thinks ideas are more important than people."—British historian Paul Johnson

"My solution to the problem (with North Vietnam) would be to tell them firmly they have to draw in their horns and stop their aggression or we're going to bomb them back into the Stone Age."—General Curtis LeMay (ret.)

"The system worked."—Secretary of Homeland Security Janet Napalitano, during a TV interview, following the Christmas Day attempt by a Nigerian terrorist to blow up an airliner landing in Detroit. She became an object of ridicule in the days that followed as the implication was that the first line of defense for U. S. flyers was to be the action of passengers leaping out of their seats to subdue a terrorist attempting to set off a bomb—and that afterwards the government's post-attack programs would kick in with clockwork efficiency and result in a system that worked—regardless of whether the plane blew up or not.

"If you want to kill any idea in the world today, get a committee working on it."—Charles Kettering

"Please don't shoot the pianist. He is doing his best."—Posted notice in a dancing saloon.

"The path you didn't take always seems smoother."—Former Secretary of Defense Donald Rumsfeld, responding to criticisms that too few troops were involved in the initial stages of the Iraq War.

"He only half dies who leaves an image of himself in his sons."—Carlo Goldoni.

"I didn't know him—but he knew me."—Weeping man watching the funeral train of President Franklin D. Roosevelt pass by, in response to a question whether he had known the president.

"One of the greatest pleasures a parent can experience is to gaze upon the children when they're fast asleep."—Unknown

"A fiery horse with the speed of light, a cloud of dust and a hearty 'Hi-yo-Silver'—the Lone Ranger."—Fred Foy, radio and television announcer, who opened The Lone Ranger radio and TV shows from 1948 to 1954, accompanied by Rossini's *William Tell Overture*. He died December 22, 2010 at age 87.

"We take the last carton of milk at the 7-11, unaware that we cause the guy behind us to drive four miles to the supermarket, where he runs into his long-lost girlfriend; they marry and have a child who grows up to discover a cure for cancer. Every day, each of us does things that move the lives of others—provoking thoughts, tipping decisions—in ways we know nothing about."—Andrew Stark, in a *Wall Street Journal* book review of *The Soul Hypothesis* by Mark C. Baker and Stewart Goetz

"The soup is terrible and the portions are too small."—from a Marx Brothers comedy routine.

"I am different now. In some ways, I think better. I am kinder, more appreciative of small things, but I am not as outgoing nor as quick to laugh. People mean well when they encourage me to get on with my life, but this is my life. . .please accept me as I am now."—From a letter by a mother who lost her 20-year old daughter in an auto accident in a letter to Dear Abby. Abby responded that "...the death of a child is the most devastating loss parents can suffer and that the experience is life changing. They may get beyond it but they never get 'over' it."

"Listening to both sides of a story will convince you that there is more to a story than both sides."—Frank Tyger

"There is only one boss: the customer. And he can fire everybody in the company, from the chairman on down, simply by spending his money someplace else."—Sam Walton, founder of Walmart.

"If you break it, you own it."—Secretary of State Colin Powell, invoking the "Pottery Barn Rule", while commenting on the invasion of Iraq by the U. S. The rule, simply stated, means that if you invade a country and overturn its government you're responsible for rebuilding the nation.

"Upward mobility from the bottom is the crux of the American promise, and the stagnation of the middle class is in fact becoming a problem, on any fair reading of the facts. Our main task is not to see that people of great wealth add to it, but that those without much money have a greater chance to earn some."—Indiana Governor Mitch Daniels

"It was probably a coincidence, but it was one of my best moments as a nurse."—Registered Nurse Barbara Dehn, relating a story in which she had recommended to a mother that she put her perfume on a diaper and hold it under the nose of her child who had been in a coma for a week, since the sense of smell is the last thing to go. The child woke up three hours later.

"I'm not moving any cot into this office. You close down the government, I'm getting' in those black SUVs with the troopers. I'm goin' to the governor's residence, gonna go upstairs, gonna open a beer, gonna order a pizza, I'm gonna watch the Mets. And when you decide to reopen the government, gimme a call, and I'll come back."—New Jersey Governor Chris Christie, in a warning to state legislators who threatened a government shut-down over proposed benefit cuts for government workers.

"On the podium before him was a stack of manila folders, one for each of our cadavers. Opening the folders, Dr. (Grant) Graves began to read to us letters written by each person before him. We learned about love, marriage, joy and family. There were moments of sadness and personal weakness. Shared with us were diseases and frailities. We shared in the stories of their lives. There were special wishes for us and special messages to us."—Paul Axelrod, M. D., Letters to the Editor, *The Wall Street Journal*, expressing his thanks to those who donated their bodies as he recalled a seminal moment in his medical education at Indiana University.

"A man over ninety is a great comfort to all his elderly neighbors: he is a picket-guard at the extreme outpost; and the young folks at sixty and seventy feel that the enemy must get by him before he can come near their camp."—Oliver Wendell Holmes

"I quote others only in order to better express myself."—Michel de Montaigne

"Americans like a winner. If you lose you're nothing."—Chessmaster Bobby Fischer, shortly before his great triumph over Russian champion Boris Spassky. Fischer subsequently ended up a loathsome caricature of himself, a fugitive without a country. "He was a celebrity ruined by his own paranoia, hubris and hatred."—*The Atlantic Monthly.* Winning isn't everything—there is much to be learned from a loss, including character development.

"What did the Foreign Office think (Libyan dictator) Colonel Gadhafi meant to do with sniper rifles and tear-gas grenades—go mole hunting?"—Britain's *Guardian* newspaper, castigating the British government for selling weapons that were being used against the Libyan people during its 2011 uprising.

"We exist today—we flourish today—not because of what *we* know we are, or what *we* know we can do, but because of what the grassroots of our country *believes* we are and *believes* we can do."—Lt. Colonel Victor Krulak, U. S. Marine Corps, leader of a group of Marine officers, who risked their careers during a fight with President Truman over a plan to eliminate the Corps, after World War II.

"What really knocks me out is a book that, when you're all done reading it, you wish the author that wrote it was a terrific friend of yours and you could call him up on the phone whenever you felt like it."—J. D. Salinger, author or the best selling, coming-of-age novel, *Catcher In The Rye*, who, paradoxically, became a recluse and avoided all contact with his readers.

"(General) Franks had to determine whether attempting to apprehend one man on the run was worth the risks."— Former Secretary of Defense Donald Rumsfeld, from his book *Known and Unknown*, attempting to explain why no specific attempt was made to capture or kill Osama Bin Laden during the opening battle in Afghanistan, during which the Taliban forces were routed and credible intelligence on Bin Laden's location was available.

"Like two skeletons copulating on a corrugated tin roof."—Thomas Beecham, British conductor, describing harpsichord music.

"The deep, deep peace of a double bed after the hurly-burly of a chaise-lounge."—Mrs. Patrick Campbell on her thoughts about her new marriage.

"Hey, where are you running? I'm one of us!"—Russian Cosmonaut Yuri Gargarin, to a forester's wife and her granddaughter, who ran away when they saw Gargarin land in a field wearing his bright orange space suit and a white helmet, after parachuting from his space capsule at the conclusion of his historic space trip in April 1961.

"I wouldn't be very smart if I screwed my way to the bottom."—Jane Seymour character to an executive who accused her of "screwing her way to the top." From the movie *Head Office.*

"Anyone who does not regularly gaze up and see the wonder and glory of a dark night filled with countless stars loses a sense of their fundamental connectedness to the universe."—Brian Greene

"A bargain is something you can't use at a price you can't resist."—Unknown

"The early bird gets the worm but the second mouse gets the cheese."—Unknown

"I hope you have developed some real intellectual curiosity. If you have it you will never, never be bored . . . To the intellectually curious the world is full of magic and full of wonder."—Marjorie Hinckley, commencement address at Brigham Young University.

"What's mine is mine, and what's yours is up for grabs."—Unknown

"Too bad all the people who know how to run the country are too busy driving taxicabs or cutting hair."—George Burns

"(North Dakota's economy) sticks out like a diamond in a bowl of cherry pits."—Ron Wirtz, editor of *fedgazette*, commenting on the precarious financial position of most states in 2011, principally due to underfunded public pension plans, high taxes, high unemployment and poor economies. North Dakota's unemployment rate was only 3.8%, as a result of a surging economy due to oil exploration and production, moderate taxes and its right-to-work status. 650 oil wells were drilled in 2010 and another 5,500 wells are planned over the next two decades. It was one of the few northern tier states to show an increase in population after several decades of decreases.

"Men occasionally stumble over the truth, but pick themselves up and hurry on as if nothing had happened."— Winston Churchill

"No Speak English, No Service. Our Staff Are Sadly Not Bi-Lingual"—Sign posted on the front door of family-owned diner in Lexington, North Carolina, after a confrontation with a group of frustrated non-English speaking Hispanics, who left in a torrent of Spanish-speaking cussing, when their order could not be understood. The sign, which had the above message, repeated in Spanish, French, Gaelic, Russian and German, resulted in a media firestorm.

"Work expands to fill the time available for its completion."—Parkinson's Law

"God is inaccessible light, surpassing every light that can be seen by us either through sense or through intellect."— Thomas Aquinas

"Looking back, I have this to regret, that too often when I loved, I did not say so."—David Grayson

"Courage is contagious. When a brave man takes a stand, the spines of others are stiffened."—Rev. Billy Graham

"Most people don't know when the best part of the day is: it's the early morning."—Harry Truman

"There will be hair and eyeballs all over the floor'"—Former Senator Alan Simpson, predicting the conflict between members of the Republican party when the move to raise the national debt limit comes to the floor of both the House and the Senate in 2011.

"You have to know the past to understand the present."—Carl Sagan

"With each choice you make, you create your life."—Unknown

"I have a dream that my four little children will one day will live in a nation where they will not be judged by the color of their skin, but by the content of their character."—Martin Luther King, Jr.

"A great civilization is not conquered from without until it has destroyed itself within. The essential causes of Rome's decline lay in her people, her morals, her class struggle, her failing trade, her bureaucratic despotism, her stifling taxes, her consuming wars."—Will Durant

"Perhaps parents would enjoy their children more if they stopped to realize that the film of childhood can never be run through for a second showing."—Evelyn Nown

"This army has seen hard times. (General) Meade and I have seen all kinds of idiots in charge, and we also know who's good. So when I tell Meade this is a good place to fight, even though he hasn't seen Gettysburg, even though I don't report directly to him, even though he's only five days on the job and in the hot seat, he takes my word. That's how things get done right in a screwed-up bureaucracy."—Union cavalryman John Buford, as related in Michael Sharra's best selling novel on the Civil War, *The Killer Angels*.

"The world hates change, yet it is the only thing that has brought progress."—Charles Kettering

"Man is equally incapable of seeing the nothingness from which he emerges and the infinity in which he is engulfed."—Blaise Pascal

"Before borrowing money from a friend, decide which you need most."—American Proverb

"Were it not for imagination, a man would be as happy in the arms of a chambermaid as of a duchess."—Dr. Samuel Johnson

"What we call the rebel force is not a force at all. It's just guys with guns."—Lt. General James Dubik (ret.), commenting on the armed group attempting to overthrow Libyan dictator, Colonel Gadhafi.

"We're in a day and age in which I can make any claim I want. I can say I believe the Buffalo Bills won the Super Bowl. Then I say it's my opinion and I have a right to it, and you're supposed to back off."—Deborah Lipstadt, Emory University professor, and author of *Denying the Holocaust: The Growing Assault on Truth and Memory.* A Gallup poll showed that 33% of Americans had some doubt that the Nazi extermination of the Jews actually happened.

"I think this is the end of the war."—Colonel Paul Tibbets, pilot of the B-29 bomber *Enola Gay*, to his copilot after completion of the mission to Hiroshima, August 6, 1945, during which the atomic bomb was dropped. The bomb, with a yield of 20,000 tons of TNT, detonated 1850 feet above the center of Hiroshima, killing 80,000 people instantly and seriously injuring another 51,000.

"*Enola Gay* has been miscast and a group of valiant Americans have had their role in history treated shamefully."—Brig. General Paul Tibbets (ret.), commenting on the proposed Smithsonian Institution's 50th anniversary commemoration of the Hiroshima bombing. The proposed exhibit cast Japan as a victim rather than as the aggressor who started the war and implied that American servicemen were little more than war criminals. The proposed exhibit ignited a firestorm of criticism upon the Smithsonian, which scrapped the controversial display and led to the resignation of the director of the Air and Space Museum. Service veterans said the display failed to reflect the sentiments and realities that existed in 1945, but instead reflected the antinuclear leanings of the museum's curators 50 years later.

"Don't compare your life to others. You have no idea what their journey is all about"—Regina Britt

"An idealist believes the short run doesn't count. A cynic believes the long run doesn't matter. A realist believes that what is done or left undone in the short run determines the long run."—Sydney J. Harris

"I once grabbed a plate of what was quite possibly turkey, but which certainly involved processed cranberry and pumpkin, in a U. S. Army position in the desert on the frontier of Iraq. It was the worst meal—by *far* the worst meal—I have ever eaten. But in all directions from the chow-hall, I could see Americans of every conceivable stripe and confession, cheerfully asserting their connection, in awful heat, with a fall of long ago. And this in a holiday that in no way could divide them. May this always be so, and may one give some modest thanks for it. "—Christopher Hitchens

"Civilizations die by suicide not by murder."—Arnold Toynbee

"What may be done at any time will be done at no time."—Scottish proverb

"If the Big Bang had been slightly less violent, the expansion of the universe would have been less rapid and soon (in a few million years or a few minutes—in any case, soon) have collapsed back on itself. If the explosion had been slightly more violent, the universe may have been dispersed into a soup too thin to aggregate into stars. The odds against us were—in just the right word—astronomical. The ratio of matter and energy to the volume of space at the Big Bang must have been within about one quadrillionth of 1 percent of ideal."—George Will

"All through the long winter, I dream of my garden. On the first day of spring, I dig my fingers into the soft earth. I can feel its energy and my spirits soar."—Helen Hayes

"The sudden abundance of low-cost natural gas is a gift."—Tim Wirth, president of the United Nations Foundation. With the introduction of a new drilling technique (hydraulic fracturing) developed in the late 1990s, immense deposits of shale gas became recoverable in the United States. The quantity of recoverable natural gas in the United States and Canada is now estimated to last 100 years—and the United States is projected to be an exporter of liquefied natural gas rather than an importer.

"Compound interest is the most powerful force in the universe."—Albert Einstein

"While women have mostly won the war for parity in men's minds, they have yet to allow themselves to believe it. And by not believing it, they restrain themselves from acting in more naturally emotional, unselfconsciously female ways that would let them be happier."—Anne Kreamer, from her book *It's Always Personal*.

"A wind blows ripples across a calm sea and those ripples, providing the wind with something to get traction on, are blown into waves."—Francisco Goldman, from his novel, *Say Her Name*, based on the death of his wife, whose neck was snapped when a large wave slammed her body on to the hard sand of a Mexican beach while she was body-surfing in shallow water.

"I love you, not only for what you are, but for what I am when I am with you."—Roy Croft

"If, in some cataclysm, all of scientific knowledge were to be destroyed, and only one sentence passed on to the next generation of creatures, what statement would contain the most information in the fewest words? I believe it is the atomic hypothesis (or the atomic fact, or whatever you wish to call it) that all things are made of atoms—little particles that move around in perpetual motion, attracting each other when they are a little distance apart, but repelling upon being squeezed into one other."—Physicist Richard Feynman

"As if you could kill time without injuring eternity."—Henry David Thoreau

"I love words but I don't like strange ones. You don't understand them and they don't understand you. Old words is like old friends—you know 'em the minute you see 'em."—Will Rogers

"There's something wonderfully inspiring about rivers—about the determination with which they set their sights on the sea and weave around the infinite obstacles in their path while never losing their sweet trilling song."—Kevin Grange, from his book on traveling within the Himalayan kingdom of Bhutan, *Beneath Blossum Rain*.

"If 9 fully loaded jumbo jets crashed every year, *something would be done about it*."—Full page newspaper ad, pointing out that 4,000 teens die in car crashes every year, supporting passage of a federal law, the STANDUP Act, that imposes restrictions on teenage drivers, such as limitations on nighttime driving. "Every day the STANDUP Act is not passed, 22 more parents will have to face the unthinkable."

"Keep your fears to yourself; share your courage with others."—Robert Louis Stevenson

"(The meeting was) marked by struggles over the agenda similar to bickering over the shape of the negotiating table."—Todd Stern, State Department official who headed the U. S. delegation at the 192 nation negotiations for a binding treaty to curb global warning held 2011 in Bangkok, Thailand. Stern said many of the participants wanted a treaty that was based on unrealistic expectations that were not doable.

"Marines run towards our bullets."—Local Afghanistan Taliban fighters yelling back at their leaders in Pakistan during a radio messages exchange, after being severely criticized for quitting a fight.

"A man never discloses his own character so clearly as when he describes another's."—Jean Paul Richter

"Let me tell you the secret that has led me to my goal. My secret lies solely in my tenacity."—Louis Pasteur

"A teacher affects eternity; he can never tell where his influence stops."—Henry Adams

"It is said that an Eastern monarch once charged his wise men to invent him a sentence, to be ever in view, and which should be true and appropriate at all times and situations. They presented him the words, 'And this, too, shall pass away'."—Abraham Lincoln

"To touch a child's face, a dog's smooth coat, a petaled flower, the rough surface of a rock, is to set up new orders of brain motion. To touch is to communicate."—James W. Angell

"Of course I'm aware of what people eating around me are looking like. I'm mostly appalled! It's amazing they get past the maitre d' . . . let alone me. I think, why aren't you at a baseball game, or eating popcorn somewhere? Anywhere but here."—Author Gay Talese, decrying the trend to casual wear in fine dining restaurants.

"They're trying to fumigate Hispanics like we're cockroaches."—Carlos Maldonado, tax preparer for Spanish speakers, on the withholding of tax refunds by states who have begun cross-checking the W-2 tax withholding forms, since many have been found to be fraudulent.

"Truth always lags behind, limping along on the arm of time."—Baltasar Gracian

"There is no silence like that of the mountains."—Guy Butler

"Very few things are as easy as they first seem."—Unknown

"All truly wise thoughts have been thought already thousands of times; but to make them truly ours, we must think them over again honestly, till they take root in our personal experience."—Goethe

"Life isn't fair but it's still good."—Regina Britt

"As soon as you trust yourself, you will know how to live."—Goethe

"A man has made at least a start in discovering the meaning of human life when he plants shade trees under which he knows he will never sit."—D. Elton Trueblood

"Do you know who are the biggest opponents of democracy in the Middle East? The husbands. As long as husbands discriminate against their wives the husbands will support the dictators."—Israeli President Shimon Peres

"If you have a show in severe decline, you're trying to catch a falling knife."— Brian Frons, head of ABC's daytime programming department, commenting on the cancellation of two of its longtime running soap operas, as opposed to making some changes in the formats to retain viewers.

"On your deathbed, what do you want to be remembered for?"—One of the interview questions asked of potential employees by Michael Mathew, CEO of YuMe, a online video advertising firm.

"If someone had said to me before I started doing this that a human being was capable of running 100 miles nonstop, I would have just said: 'No way. I mean, how?"—Dean Karnazes, an ultramarathon runner, on the 35th day of his projected 2,900 mile 75-day run across the United States.

"We are all mortal until the first kiss and the second glass of wine."—Eduardo Galeano

"TRY TO BREAK IN THIS HOUSE AGAIN, YOUR HEAD WILL BE BLOWN OFF."— Large sign posted in front of a Texas home, after an attempted house invasion the previous night.

"I know I have the body of a weak and feeble woman but I have the heart and stomach of a King and of a King of England, too. . . . rather than any dishonor shall grow by me, I myself will take up arms."—Queen Elizabeth I to the English Army assembled to meet the expected Spanish army aboard the Armada headed for England's shore (1588).

"Being noosed with 'most likely to succeed' is like lugging an albatross to every job interview, new relationship or writing endeavor."—Blake Atwood, copywriter for a law firm, on the dubious honor bestowed on him by the high school graduating class yearbook. Nearly one-third of those named "most likely" in high school regard it later as "a curse" according to a recent poll of 1,369 members of MemoryLane.com. Schools are veering away from such designations, including those of a disparaging nature, such as "most likely to have a conversation with himself", based on legal considerations.

"No nation occupies a foot of land that was not stolen."—Mark Twain

"The heart of a mother is a deep abyss at the bottom of which you will always find forgiveness."—Honore de Balzac

"When I am getting ready to reason with a man, I spend one third of my time thinking about myself and what I am going to say and two thirds about him and what he is going to say."—Abraham Lincoln

"There are only two ways to live your life. One is as though nothing is a miracle. The other is as though everything is a miracle."—Albert Einstein

"Pick battles big enough to matter, small enough to win."—Jonathan Kozel

"I have seen the future, and it works."—Lincoln Steffens, American muckraking investigative reporter and hater of capitalism, upon returning from Soviet Russia in 1919, then in the midst of the Bolshevik revolution, which he described as "very, very beautiful."

"Come on, Lakotas. It's a good day to die."—Chief Crazy Horse to his Sioux warriors, as he led them into battle against General Custer's troops at the Little Big Horn.

"The strong do what they can, and the weak suffer what they must."—Maxim of ancient warfare, that is just as applicable to modern warfare.

"I ain't got no quarrel with them Viet Cong. Why me?"—Boxer Muhammed Ali, commenting on the cancellation of his draft deferment during the Vietnam War. He followed up these comments with a suggestion that the government should draft poor boys, who didn't pay as much in taxes to buy guns and tanks, as he did.

"No problem can withstand the assault of sustained thinking."—Voltaire

"Don't tread on me."—Motto on first official American flag, that pictured a snake, flown by Lt. John Paul Jones. This motto was appropriated by many involved in the Tea Party movement in 2010.

"Gold and love affairs are difficult to hide."—Spanish proverb

"When they come here a lot of them don't know how to flush a toilet. One of the first things they do is go in the dumpster and eat. O. K.? That's the kind of people you have there."—Daniel Bruckner, owner of squalid, cockroach-infested apartments being rented to Burmese refugees, in response to criticisms leveled at him in news reports.

"This is the work I loved most, this intimate contact with the four men."—Gutzon Borglum, creator and chief sculptor of the Mount Rushmore sculpture, which was begun October, 1927 and continued until his death in 1941. The sculpture of four presidents involved a workforce of 400 men, who blasted away 450,000 tons of granite, 90% by dynamite and 10% by jackhammer.

"A smile is an inexpensive way to improve your looks."—Charles Gordy

"You're going to learn that one of the most brutal things in the world is your average nineteen year old American boy."—Philip Caputo

"And when he goes to heaven,
  To Saint Peter he will tell,
  Another Marine reporting, sir;
  I've served my time in hell!"
--Grave epitaph for PFC Cameron of the Marine Corps, Guadacanal,1942.

"One of the bravest men I saw in the African campaign was at the top of a telegraph pole in the midst of furious fire as we were plowing towards Tunis. I stopped and asked him what in the hell he was doing there at a time like that. He answered, 'Fixing the wire, sir.' Isn't it a little unhealthy right now, I asked. 'Yes, sir, but this God damn wire has got to be fixed."—General George Patton

"Politics in a novel resembles nothing so much as a pistol fired in the theater—a terrible disruption, but it does get one's attention."—Stendhal

"Water cannot be destroyed. In fact every molecule of water on the planet has been here since the beginning, or about 4.4 billion years. The water you drink from a Dasani bottle probably passed through the kidney of a dinosaur."—Charles Fishman, from his book *The Big Thirst: The Secret Life and Turbulent Future of Water*

"I can feel guilty about the past, apprehensive about the future, but only in the present can I act. The ability to be in the present moment is a major component of mental wellness."—Abraham Maslow

"One way to get high blood pressure is to go mountain climbing over molehills."—Earl Wilson

"There were three of us in this marriage, so it was a bit crowded."—Princess Diana, commenting on her husband's relationship with Camilla Bowes, during a BBC interview.

"If we do discover a complete (unified) theory (of the universe) it should, in time, be understandable, in broad principle, by everyone, not just a few scientists. Then we shall all . . . be able to take part in the discussion of why it is that we and the universe exist. If we find the answer to that, It would be the ultimate triumph of human reason, for then we should know the mind of God."—Stephen Hawking, author of *A Brief History Of Time*

"Keep this saying before your eyes: 'It is not fitting for a Prophet that he should have prisoners of war until he hath thoroughly subdued the land. Therefore when you meet the unbelievers (in fight) smite them on their necks'."—Osama bin Laden, advocating the execution of all prisoners by beheading.

"In a hierarchy every employee rises to the level of his incompetence."—The Peter Principle

"Somebody had to do something for suffering humanity. I put myself in my patients' place. This is something I would want."—Dr. Jack Kevorkian, also known as "Doctor Death", who assisted in the suicide/murder of 130 people who were suffering from incurable cancer, Lou Gehrig's disease or multiple sclerosis.

"Actually, it's a lot of fun to fight. You know, it's a hell of a hoot . . . it's fun to shoot some people. I'll be right up front with you. I like brawling. You go into Afghanistan, you got guys who slap women around for five years because they don't got no manhood left anyway, so it's a hell of a lot of fun to shoot them."—Marine Lt. General James Mattis. These remarks resulted in a public reprimand to the general from his superiors.

"You've never lived until you've almost died. For those who fight for it, life has a meaning the protected will never know."—Leigh Wade

"If I could save the Union without freeing *any* slave I would do it, and if I could save it by freeing *all* the slaves I would do it; and if I could save it by freeing some and leaving others alone I would also do that."—President Abraham Lincoln

"I wish that I owned every slave in the South, I would free them all to avoid this war."—Robert E. Lee

"That image comes back to me every day."—Former New York Mayor Rudolph Guliani, of his witnessing of two people, hand in hand, jumping from the World Trade Center, on September 11, 2001.

"Never give in—never… never… never."—Sir Winston Churchill, in a commencement address he gave at Harrow, the prep school he attended as a young boy.

"Everybody on this planet is separated by only six other people. Six degrees of separation between us and everybody else on the planet."—John Guare

"It struck beside me with a noise like a house falling . . . I must have shut my eyes, for when I opened them again I was in a world of fairyland. On every tree in the garden below, and on every tree so far as the eyes could see some sort of blazing oil had fallen, and it was dancing on the trees and branches with a million little red and yellow candle-flames. On the ground in between the trees and in all the open spaces, white balls of fire had fallen, and these were bouncing like tennis balls, high in the air to the tree tops, and down and up again."—Father Gustav Bitter, describing his experience during the bombing of Tokyo on the night of April 15, 1945. On this night 1,930 tons of incendiary bombs, filled with napalm, were dropped by American B-29 bombers, burning out six square miles of the city. From the book *Commander In Chief: Franklin Delano Roosevelt* by Eric Larrabee.

"Take that woman out and do not let her in again."—Secretary of War Edward Stanton, speaking of Mary Lincoln, whose screaming and wailing at the bedside of her husband, the dying President Lincoln, in a bedroom in the Peterson house across from Ford's Theater, unnerved everyone, especially Stanton.

"Rest is not idleness, and to lie sometimes on the grass on a summer day listening to the murmur of water, or watching the clouds float across the sky, is hardly a waste of time."—John Lubbock. And if we can't enjoy these moments in life, what's the point of living.

"Never stop learning. If you learn one new thing every day, you will overcome 99% of your competition."—Joe Carlozo

"I love the smell of napalm in the morning. It smells like . . . victory!" — Robert Duvall's commanding officer's character, after witnessing a napalm bombing of a Viet Cong position. From the movie *Apocalypse Now*.

"Let there be no more bloodshed between Arabs and Israelis."—Anwar al-Sadat, President of Egypt, as he signed the Egyptian-Israeli peace treaty on March 26, 1979. Two years later he was assassinated by Muslim extremists.

"It ended so quickly we fell off the cliff."—Lou Glazer, president of Michigan Future, lamenting the economic plunge of the state during the period 2000-2010. Michigan and Ohio were the only two states to show negative growth during that period.

"Hellacious."—James Arthur Ray, self-help guru, describing the expected experience of "Spiritual Warrior" participants in a 2009 Arizona sweat lodge ordeal he was encouraging them to endure, even though they would feel like they were dying. He was found guilty of three counts of negligent homicide when the ceremony, involving 50 people, ended in chaos, with participants vomiting, shaking and being dragged from the sweat lodge. In addition to the three deaths, eighteen others had to be hospitalized.

"With all due respect, it's none of your business."—New Jersey governor Chris Christie, to a questioner from the audience who asked why the governor did not send his children to public schools.

"In peace, sons bury their fathers. In war, fathers bury their sons."—Herodotus

"Chris (Krzysztof Walenczak, Poland's under secretary of state at the Ministry of Treasury), shared with us fascinating insights on how Poland has successfully sold off 500 (state) entities, with plans to sell off another 300 fairly soon. But not a single person from the Greek government was there to learn from the Poles' experience—and that in a nutshell, is why Greece is falling apart."—Steve Forbes in *Forbes Magazine*

"He who asks a question may be a fool for five minutes; he who never asks a question remains a fool forever."—Unknown

"The pessimist complains about the wind; the optimist expects it to change; the realist adjusts the sails."—William Arthur Ward

"Find something to laugh about."—Maya Angelou

"If anything happened to that man, I couldn't stand it. He is the truest friend, he has the farthest vision; he is the greatest man I have ever known."—British Prime Minister Winston Churchill to Kenneth Pendar, the evening's dinner host, as President Franklin D. Roosevelt's plane left Morocco, following their wartime conference in Casablanca, in January 1943. From Eric Larrabee's book *Commander In Chief: Franklin Delano Roosevelt.*

"So, he died."—Stephen Ambrose, from his book *Citizen Soldiers*, recounting a story of a young captured German SS sergeant who shunned a blood transfusion when he could not be assured that there was no Jewish blood in it.

"They were called movies—and I made them move."—Film director Raoul Walsh, known for some of the best action movies to come out of Warner Brothers during its hey-day in the 40s and 50s, such as *High Sierra, They Died With Their Boots On* and *White Heat.* Jack Warner, head of production, said, "Raoul's idea of a tender love scene is to burn down a whorehouse."

"The soldier's trade, if it is to mean anything at all, has to be anchored to an unshakeable code of honor. Otherwise, those of us who follow the drums become nothing more than a bunch of hired assassins walking around in gaudy clothes . . . a disgrace to God and mankind."—German Major General Carl von Clausewitz, 1832. One wonders what his thoughts would have been regarding the SS soldiers in charge of the extermination camps during World War II.

"Physically, they are good assets. Financially, they are all black holes."—Ding Yuan, accounting professor at the China Europe International Business School in Shanghai, commenting on the $300 billion high speed rail network under construction in China. The 180 mph train between Beijing and Shanghai, runs half empty due to the high cost of a ticket—approximately $86, about 9% of the average monthly disposable income of a Chinese citizen.

"My God! I am so lucky to be living in the Soviet Union."—Borya, a young Muscovite prior to the breakup of the Soviet Union, when told of the riots and shootings in the West. Years later, as a teacher, Borya taught students about the horrors of the Soviet past—the collectivization, the deportations, and the gulags. From a PBS program *My Perestroika.*

"The photograph of the flag being raised on Iwo Jima means the continued existence of the Marine Corps for the next five hundred years."—Secretary of the Navy James Forrestal's pronouncement to Marine General Archer Vandergrift

"There are three kinds of people; those that make things happen, those that watch things happen and those who don't know what's happening."—American proverb

"If you call a tail a leg, how many legs does a dog have? Four, because a tail is not a leg, even if you call it one."—President Abraham Lincoln

"Make yourself necessary to somebody."—Ralph Waldo Emerson

"He can run but he can't hide."—Boxer Joe Louis before his heavyweight title fight against Billy Conn (June 19, 1946).

"A minute earlier he had been the most powerful man in the world. Upon his word the fate of millions of men, not to mention great nations, depended. The moment he uttered the word, however, he was powerless. For the next two or three days there was almost nothing he could do that would in any way change anything. The invasion could not be stopped, not by him, not by anyone . . . He could now only sit and wait."—Stephen Ambrose from his book *Supreme Commander*, describing the decision of General Dwight D. Eisenhower, in the face of unstable weather conditions, to initiate the invasion of Europe on D-Day, June 6, 1944.

"There is always inequity in life. Some men are killed in war and some men are wounded, and some men never leave the country . . . Life is unfair."—John F. Kennedy

"Lie to me. Tell me all these years you've been waiting. Tell me."—from the movie *Johnny Guitar*, spoken by Sterling Hayden.

"People have got to know whether or not their president is a crook. Well I'm not a crook."—President Richard Nixon at a press conference November 11, 1973, nine months before resigning due to the Watergate scandal.

"Don't sell the steak; sell the sizzle."—Elmer Wheeler

"At Sixty Miles An Hour the Loudest Noise in the New Rolls Royce Came From the Electric Clock."—David Oglivy, citing the best advertising headline he ever wrote. From *Confessions of an Advertising Man*.

"Explain to me how an Apache brave can chase down a runaway mustang and I've got kids who get tired playing basketball."—Coach Abe Lemons

"He deserved it."—Yankee fan Christian Lopez, speaking to the press, after handing the homerun ball he caught to Yankee Derek Jeter, representing the 3000th hit of Jeter's career. Lopez was scoffed at by some New Yorkers, for not putting the ball up for auction, which could have probably fetched a bid of $250,000. CNN, obviously confused by the event, ran a ribbon headline on its screen saying, "Derek Jeter gets 3000th homer."

"They have sown the wind, and now they are going to reap the whirlwind."—World War II British Air Marshal Arthur "Bomber" Harris, describing his intended use of massive bomber fleets in night operations against Germany, in retaliation for the German bombing of British cities. An estimated 600,000 Germans were killed in the bombing of German cities, many of which were reduced to rubble at war's end, by both American and British bombers.

"Efficiency is doing things right; effectiveness is doing the right things."—Peter Drucker

"Feeling sorry for yourself, and your present condition, is not only a waste of energy but the worst habit you could possibly have."—Dale Carnegie

"Go confidently in the direction of your dreams. Live the life you have imagined."—Henry David Thoreau

" . . . an elemental force freed from its bonds after being chained for billions of years."—William Laurence, describing the first atomic bomb blast in the New Mexico desert.

"Good on you, sport."—Passing Australian soldiers grasping the outstretched skeleton hand of a Japanese soldier embedded in the mud who had died in the disastrous Japanese retreat over the Owen Stanley Mountains in New Guinea during World War II. From William Manchester's book, *Goodbye Darkness*.

"No man crosses the same river twice, because the river has changed, and so has the man."—Heraclitus

"You love me so much, you want to put me in your pocket. And I should die there smothered."—D. H. Lawrence, from his novel *Sons and Lovers*.

"President Obama, this is your army. We are ready to march. Let's take these son-of-bitches out and give America back to an America where we belong."—Teamsters President Jimmy Hoffa Jr. at a rally for the president, a few months after the president had called for more civility in political discourse following the shooting of Arizona Representative Gabrielle Giffords by a deranged gunman. President Obama came to the stage minutes later and made no comment on Hoffa's statement.

"The unleashed power of the atom has changed everything except our modes of thinking, and we thus drift toward unparalleled catastrophes".— Albert Einstein

"Former Vice President Al Gore went on a profanity-laced tirade at the Aspen Institute August 4 (2011) against the rising number of Americans who are skeptical about man-made global warming. . . Global temperatures peaked in 1998. People have noticed winters are getting colder. . . Polar ice caps are larger. So is the polar bear population. . . The rise in sea levels—which has been going on since the end of the last ice age—is slowing down. . . His credibility is in tatters. In the public mind, he's gone from Nobel Prize winner to Chicken Little."—Jack Kelly, in a column in the *Pittsburgh Post-Gazette*.

"If I had eight hours to chop down a tree, I'd spend six hours sharpening my ax."—Abraham Lincoln

"I never saw a wild thing sorry for itself."—D. H. Lawrence

"Democrats believe in the welfare state before they believe in capitalism. The assumption is that there is some kind of perpetual engine of economic prosperity in America that is just going to continue. And therefore they are able to take from those who create and give it to those who don't."—Republican Eric Cantor, House Majority Leader

"Elections have consequences, and Eric, I won."—President Barak Obama, to Republican Eric Cantor, after Cantor put forth the Republican view of actions to be taken to reinvigorate the U. S. economy, shortly after Obama won the presidency.

"I want the people of America to work less for the government and more for themselves. I want them to have the rewards of their own industry. That is the chief meaning of freedom."— President Calvin Coolidge

"A cadet will not lie, cheat, steal or tolerate those who do."—The honor code of the Army cadet corps at West Point.

"When the shepherd speaks well of the wolf, the sheep are in trouble."—Unknown

"This means to the average person you're better off in the casket than doing the eulogy."—Jerry Seinfeld, commenting on the fact that many people fear public speaking more than death.

"Every man builds his world in his own image. He has the power to choose, but no power to escape the necessity of choice."—Ayn Rand

"Hayden, get a job!"—Peter Fonda, roaring up to the home of Tom Hayden and Jane Fonda, on his motorcycle. Hayden, who spent most of his time meeting with his friends promoting left-wing causes, lived off the earnings of his wife, during their marriage. From the book *Jane Fonda: The Private Life of a Public Woman*, by Patricia Bosworth.

"I appreciate everyone's support, but it was by my own personal diligence, that I won it, after all."—Chinese tennis player, Li Na, at a press conference, after winning the French Open. Miffed at her lack of thanks to her country, the Chinese Propaganda Ministry ordered domestic media to keep a lid on their praise of her. "Do not continue to hype Li Na's win."

"If a man hasn't discovered something he will die for, he isn't fit to live."—Martin Luther King Jr.

"If you lose your footing, powerful currents will carry you over the falls. There's no second chance."—Warning sign posted near Vernal Falls at Yosemite National Park. In July, 2011 two men and a woman were swept over the 317-foot falls while wading in the Merced River beyond a fenced barrier.

"The physician can bury his mistakes, but the architect can only advise his client to plant vines."—Frank Lloyd Wright

"I don't know if (his statement) was a publicity thing or if someone had just peed in his bowl of cereal that morning and he was mad."—TV cook Paula Deen, responding to a comment by Anthony Bourdain that her butter-loving cooking made her "the worst, most dangerous person in America."

"There is no other way to put it—they exploded."—Witness on 9/11, describing the impact of falling bodies on some of the firemen entering the Twin Towers. Bodies rained down by the score as the flames became unbearable to the workers in the in the upper floors. As the workers streamed out of the towers from the lower floors firemen were going the other way—343 never returned.

"There is hardly anything in the world that some man cannot make a little worse and sell a little cheaper, and the people who consider price only are this man's lawful prey."—John Ruskin. This quotation was engraved on a sign in the outer office of Dore Shary, head of production of Metro-Goldwyn-Mayer in the early 1950s.

"Never praise a sister to a sister in the hope of your compliments reaching the proper ear."—Rudyard Kipling

"A few of the trains slipped past Hiroshima. Virtually every POW believed that the destruction of the city had saved them from execution. John Falconer, a survivor of the Bataan Death March, looked out as Hiroshima neared. 'First there were the trees,' he told historian Donald Knox. 'Then the leaves were missing. As you got closer branches were missing. Closer still the trunks were gone, and then, as you got in the middle, there was nothing. Nothing! It was beautiful. I realized this is what ended the war. It meant we didn't have to go hungry any longer, or without medical treatment. I was so insensitive to anyone else's human needs and suffering. I know it's not right to say it was beautiful, because it really wasn't. But I believed the end probably justified the means'."—From *Unbroken* by Laura Hillenbrand. The war ended roughly a week before the Japanese planned to execute all remaining Allied POWs, approximately 100,000, in anticipation of invasion of their home islands. About 25% of the prisoners had already died due to malnutrition, beatings, lack of medical treatment and execution.

"Talent alone won't make you a success. Neither will being in the right place at the right time, unless you are ready. The most important question is: 'Are you ready?'"—Johnny Carson

"Every creature is better alive than dead—men and moose and pine trees, and he who understands that will rather preserve its life than destroy it."—Henry David Thoreau

"There are four ways, and only four ways, in which we have contact with the world. We are evaluated and classified by these four contacts: what we do, how we look, what we say, and how we say it."—Dale Carnegie

"Courage is the first of human qualities because it is the quality that guarantees all the others."—Winston Churchill

"Next time I send some dumb son-of-a-bitch for a Coca Cola, I go myself."—Movie director Michael Curtiz, who constantly mangled the English language, complaining, on the set, about the tardiness of a gofer he had sent to get him a Coke.

"They should stop swatting flies and go after the manure pile."—Retired General Curtis LeMay, advocating military strikes on North Vietnam early in the war.

"An expert is one who knows more and more about less and less."—Nicholas Butler

"Opportunities are usually disguised as hard work, so most people don't recognize them."—Ann Landers

"If you're alive, there's a purpose for your life. You were made by God and for God, and until you understand that, life will never make sense."—Rick Warren, church founder and author of "A Purpose Driven Life".

"Those who stand for nothing fall for anything."—Alexander Hamilton

"Reading is a means of thinking with another person's mind; it forces you to stretch your own."—Charles Scribner, Jr.

"She plucked from my lapel the invisible strand of lint (the universal act of woman to proclaim ownership)."—O. Henry (William Sydney Porter)\

"Thou shall not speak ill of a fellow Republican."—Ronald Reagan, putting forth his 11th Commandment for Republicans.

"If you bungle raising your children nothing else much matters in life."—Jackie Kennedy

"But the real edge lies with culture, particularly the English language, which has decimated all its traditional competition—French, German and Russian—over the past two decades. Difficult to learn, Chinese is not likely to replace English any time soon as the dominant language of culture, air travel, science and technology."—Joel Korkin

"When you reach the end of your rope, tie a knot in it and hang on."—Thomas Jefferson

"The president has to be someone who can persuade the American people to do what they don't want to do and to like it."—President Harry Truman

"Death is the destination we all share."—Apple founder Steve Jobs at a commencement address to Stanford graduates.

"Love comes when manipulation stops; when you think more about the other person than about his or her reactions to you. When you dare to reveal yourself fully. When you dare to be vulnerable."—Joyce Brothers

"Too often we underestimate the power of a touch, a smile, a kind word, a listening ear, an honest compliment, or the smallest act of caring, all of which have the potential to turn a life around."—Leo Buscaglia

"The line between failure and success is so fine that we scarcely know when we pass it: so fine that we are often on the line and do not know it."—Elbert Hubbard

"The best way to be boring is to leave nothing out."—Voltaire

"There are two things people want more than sex and money... recognition and praise."—Mary Kay Ash

"If a small thing has the power to make you angry, does that not indicate something about your size?"—Sydney J. Harris

"There is no pillow so soft as a clear conscience."—French Proverb

"The trouble with not having a goal is that you can spend your life running up and down the field and never scoring."—Bill Copeland

"Live your dreams one step at a time."—Inscription written on a World MS flag held by Lori Schneider, resident of Bayfield, Wisconsin, and afflicted with multiple sclerosis, during a photo taken on top of Mount Everest in July 2009. Lori, the first person with multiple sclerosis to climb Mount Everest, presented the flag to the Multiple Sclerosis International offices in London as an inspiration to all those suffering from the disease.

"It doesn't matter what he does, he will never amount to anything."—one of Albert Einstein's teachers to Albert's dad.

"You know it's going to hell when the best rapper out there is white and the best golfer is black."—Charles Barkley

"No man would listen to you talk, if he didn't know it was his turn next."—E. W. Howe

"This is all you have. This is not a dry run. This is your life. If you want to fritter it away with your fears, then you will fritter it away, but you won't get it back later."—Laura Schlessinger

"The Marines I have seen around the world have the cleanest bodies, the filthiest minds, the highest morale, and the lowest morals of any group of animals I have ever seen. Thank God for the United States Marine Corps!"— Eleanor Roosevelt, First Lady of the United States, 1945

"Consider the overconfidence bias, which drives many of our mistakes in decision-making. The best demonstration of the bias comes from the world of investing. . . the year-to-year correlation between the performance of the vast majority of funds is barely above zero, which suggests that most successful managers are banking on luck, not talent. This shouldn't be too surprising. The stock market is a case study in randomness, a system so complex that it's impossible to predict. Nevertheless, professional investors routinely believe that they can see what others can't. The end result is that they make far too many trades, with costly consequences."—Daniel Kahneman, from his book *Thinking, Fast and Slow*

". . .we might well have viewed it as an act of war."—Excerpt from a Department of Education report, issued in the 1980's, citing our possible response if a foreign power had imposed upon the United States our mediocre educational system. From a speech by Rupert Murdoch.

"In playing ball, and in life, a person occasionally gets the opportunity to do something great. When that time comes, only two things matter: being prepared to seize the moment and having the courage to take your best swing."—Hank Aaron

"I do not object to people looking at their watches when I am speaking. But I strongly object when they start shaking them to see if they're still going."—Lord Birkett

"Marines die, that's what we're here for. But the Marine Corps lives forever. And that means that <u>you</u> live forever."—Marine Gunnery Sgt. Hartman, portrayed by R. Lee Ermey, a former Marine Corps Drill Instructor, using his own choice of words in *Full Metal Jacket*.

"One of the biggest problems plaguing our society is the legions of adult demanding to be treated like babies. The country of 'rugged individualism' is now inundated with whiny, money-grubbing complainants suing the deepest pockets for every innocuous discomfort to which they are subjected, ranging from coffee burns ($2.8 million), to in-flight turbulence, to a two cent discrepancy in a product refund. . . The root of frivolous lawsuits is greed coupled with a failure to take responsibility for one's own actions."—Rachel Bodner, in a Letter to the Editor in *The Wall Street Journal*.

"I come in peace, I didn't bring artillery. But I am pleading with you with tears in my eyes: If you fuck with me, I'll kill you all."—Marine General James Mattis, to Iraqi tribal leaders

"Never, never waste a minute on regret. It's a waste of time."—Harry S. Truman

"One of the most important lessons Dad taught us is not to feel like victims. He never felt like a victim, he never talked like a victim. And both of our parents taught not to think that the government owed us something. They didn't teach us to be mad at this country."—Herman Cain

"Anyone who keeps the ability to see beauty never grows old."—Author Franz Kafka

"(Senator) Hubert Humphrey talks so fast that listening to him is like trying to read *Playboy* with your wife turning the pages."—Senator Barry Goldwater

"Sometimes doing your best isn't good enough. Sometimes you need to do what is required."—Winston Churchill

"Before finalizing a decision, imagine a year after it has been made, that it has turned out horribly, then write a history of how it went wrong and why."—From the book *Thinking, Fast and Slow* by Daniel Kahneman, describing "pre-mortem", an exercise developed by psychologist Gary Klein to avoid overconfidence when starting a large project or preparing a forecast.

"I like Bloomberg, he's a friend. But fuck him and the salt. I like salt. It's not his business."—Roger Ailes, founder of Fox News, commenting on the "food war" conducted by New York Mayor Michael Bloomberg seeking to eliminate excess salt in fast food and restaurant meals, including removing salt packets and shakers from tables.

"Your soul may belong to God, but your ass belongs to the Army."—Greeting by drill sergeants to new recruits.

"The real class war that threatens us is a class of bureaucrats and connected crony capitalists trying to rise above the rest of us, call the shots, rig the rules and preserve their place atop society."—Rep. Paul Ryan

"Instead of appealing to the hope and optimism that were hallmarks of his first campaign, he has launched his second campaign by preying on the emotions of fear, envy and resentment."—Rep. Paul Ryan, on the reelection tactics of President Obama.

"UNABLE TO OBTAIN BIDET. SUGGEST HANDSTAND IN SHOWER."—Telegram sent by Director Billy Wilder to his wife, who had asked him to buy her a bidet when he was in Paris.

"I was instantly suspicious. Remembering what my father had told me about spotting untrustworthy men, I had hit the jackpot here. Two of them had beards, one was wearing sandals and another one had a bow tie. The only thing missing were the two-toned shoes. The object of my free love had disappeared and here I was with a group of guys who obviously so far had not done very well in the redistribution of wealth by the look of them. One of them put a form on the desk in front of me and told me to sign it and pay over my subscription of five shillings. I saw at once what a mistake I had made: the distribution of wealth was to be mine to them, not the other way around. I fled—and a lingering suspicion of Communism has remained planted in my mind forever."—From actor Michael Caine's autobiography, *What's It All About*, describing his enticement to a small dingy office by an attractive older woman who gave him a leaflet published by the Young Communists calling for the redistribution of wealth.

"You ain't goin' nowhere, son. You ought to go back to drivin' a truck."—Jim Denny, firing Elvis Presley after one performance on Grand Ole Opry.

"Who are these 30%?"—Sean Hannity, citing a poll on the Occupy Wall Street demonstrations, which had the public turning against them 39% to 31%, with another 30% stating they didn't know enough about the well-publicized demonstrations—almost two months after they started. You have to wonder whether some people just wander through life in a cloud, oblivious to what's happening in the world.

"If I am to speak for ten minutes, I need a week for preparation; if fifteen minutes, three days; if half an hour, two days; if an hour, I am ready now."—Woodrow Wilson

"Inventions have long since reached their limit, and I see no hope for further developments."—Roman engineer Julius Sextus Frontinus in 10 A. D.

"Everything that can be invented has been invented."—Charles Duell, Commissioner of U. S. Patent Office, 1899, in a report to President McKinley, recommending that his office be abolished.

"Most people feed it to the pigs."—Sonia Martinez, a Hawaii-based food writer, describing her thoughts on breadfruit, a nutritious and energy packed food that, unfortunately, is almost tasteless and some compare to undercooked potatoes. Its transfer from the South Pacific to the Caribbean was the objective of the infamous trip of the *HMS Bounty* to Tahiti in 1787.

"Four feet high, covered, except in the face, with short, glossy, copper-colored hair (they had batlike) wings composed of a thin membrane, without hair, lying snugly upon their backs from the top of their shoulders to the calves of their legs."—Excerpt from a report published by the *New York Sun* in 1835 on the extraordinary findings of Sir John Herschel, a leading astronomer, when he examined the moon using a revolutionary telescope with a 24-foot lens and found it inhabited with strange animals including the one described above. The report caused a sensation in 19th century New York, before it was exposed as a fraud when Mr. Herschel disclaimed all knowledge of such findings.

"Occupy Everything, Death to Capitalism." —Large black banner carried by protesters in Oakland, California. My question is "Why are they here?" They should all be applying for visas to go to North Korea, the anti-capitalist paradise of their dreams.

"When you're with someone who is dying, try to get in bed and snuggle with them. Often they feel very alone and just want to be touched. Many times my patients will tell me, 'I'm living with cancer but dying from lack of affection.'"—Registered nurse Barbara Dehn

"The 442nd (Regimental Combat Team) experienced some of the most horrific fighting in Europe and became the most-decorated unit in U. S. military history for its size and length of service. In just 10 months of combat, more than 700 were killed or listed as missing in action."—from an article by Kevin Freking in *The Arizona Republic*, describing the valor of the unit that was composed entirely of Japanese-Americans during World War II, most of whose family members spent much of the war in U. S. internment camps, since they were considered security risks.

"There is no democracy without irreverence."—French Minister of Culture Frederic Mitterand, speaking out in support of the Paris-based satirical magazine *Charlie Hebdo* after it suffered a fire caused by a Molotov cocktail shortly after it published caricatures of Muhammad.

"I simply do not know where the money is."—Former CEO of MF Global Jon Corzine, in testimony to a House Committee investigating the disappearance of over $1 billion in customer account money at the firm. Has anyone looked in the petty cash drawer? After all, it's only a billion dollars.

"If you can't say something good about someone, sit right here by me."—Written in needlepoint on a throw pillow of Alice Roosevelt Longworth, lover of gossip, daughter of President Theodore Roosevelt.

"Men make history and not the other way around. In periods where there is no leadership, society stands still. Progress occurs when courageous, skillful leaders seize the opportunity to change things for the better."— President Harry Truman

"For the (atheistic) scientist who has lived by his faith in the power of reason, the story ends like a bad dream. He has scaled the mountains of ignorance; he is about to conquer the highest peak; as he pulls himself over the final rock, he is greeted by a band of theologians who have been sitting there for centuries."— Astronomer Robert Jastrow, commenting on the discovery that the universe was created in a "Big Bang" 14 billion years ago from nothing, with the only possible answer being creation by a supernatural outside force.

"The future belongs to people who see possibilities before they become obvious."—Ted Levitt

"People didn't start breeding like rabbits; they stopped dying like flies."—Nicholas Eberstadt, a demographer, citing the major reason for the increase in the earth's population, from an estimated 300 million in the Roman era to seven billion in 2011, primarily due to major advances in nutrition and medicine. Whereas the average life span during the Roman era was about 25 years it is currently in the mid-70s and projected to rise. It is not unusual to find four generations of a family group living today.

"When I was a boy of 14, my father was so ignorant I could hardly stand to have him around. But when I got to be 21 I was astonished at how much the old man had learned in seven years."—Mark Twain

"Now I think I'll take a swig of the 10-year old package of Alka Seltzer in my medicine chest to ease the nausea I'm feeling from calculating how many billions of dollars the pharmaceutical industry bilks out of unknowing consumers every year who discard perfectly good drugs and buy new ones because they trust the industry's expiration date labeling."—Richard Altschuler, self-appointed investigator of the expiration dates on OTC and prescription medications, after finding that testing, conducted by the US Food and Drug Administration (FDA), ultimately covering more than 100 drugs, showed that about 90% of them were safe and effective as far as 15 years past their expiration date.

"As some have pointed out recently, if you can keep your head when all around are losing theirs, it's just possible you haven't grasped the situation."—Jean Kerr

"The explosion would have been the equivalent of two million hydrogen bombs."—Matt Ridley, describing the power of the large meteor that struck the earth off the coast of the Yucatan Peninsula of Mexico in the Gulf of Mexico, 65 million years ago, causing a 110 mile wide crater, and thought to be the cause of a massive die-off of the dinosaurs and two thirds of the other animal and plant species on the earth.

"A commonsense interpretation of the facts suggests that a superintellect has monkeyed with physics, as well as chemistry and biology, and that there are no blind forces worth speaking about in nature."—Physicist Fred Hoyle, commenting on the conclusion he reached after studying the complexities of life, the "Big Bang" and the many laws of physics which are tuned "just right" to allow for the existence of the universe.

"Today's gridlock . . . is the result of a fiscal crisis and the fact that Republicans finally are prepared to challenge the welfare-state vision. Democrats and blue-state voters deeply believe in their model and intend to see it completed. Republicans and red-state voters want to engineer a U-turn that restores a land-of-opportunity model rather than a nanny state. Both parties recognize that the U. S. is very close to a point of no-return, with more and more citizens relying on government payouts. . . That debate is healthy, long overdue and extremely painful"—Tom West, in a Letter to the Editor in *The Wall Street Journal*.

"Seven months ago I could give a single command and 541,000 people would immediately obey it. Today I can't get a plumber to come to my house.—Former General H. Norman Schwarzkopf, Supreme Commander of Allied Forces in the Persian Gulf War.

"Art begins where the 'tiny bit' begins."—Russian painter Karl Bryullov, after he had made a minor change in a student's sketch, eliciting the comment, "Why you only changed it a tiny bit." Leo Tolstoy, in an essay commented, "That saying is strikingly true not only of art but of all life. One may say that true life begins where the 'tiny bit' (of change in one's life) begins." From the book, *Tolstoy: A Russian Life*, by Rosamund Bartlett.

"Markets can remain irrational far longer than you or I can remain solvent."—British economist John Maynard Keynes, commenting on the fact that although individual investors may be correct in their evaluation of a market security or condition, they cannot overcome the irrational mass action of other participants in the market.

"The paradox is that the welfare state, designed to improve security and dampen social conflict, now looms as an engine for insecurity, conflict and disappointment. Facing the hard questions of finding a sustainable balance between individual protections and better economic growth, the Europeans have spent years dawdling. The parallel with our situation is all too obvious."—Robert J. Samuelson, *Washington Post*

"We see them as super-cool because they look like they're having fun. With the Americans, it comes from the heart."—Alexandra Meissnitzer, former Austrian World Cup champion, commenting on the fact that the U. S. is producing skiers who are consistently landing on the podiums at World Cup events as never before.

"The government decides to try to increase the middle class by subsidizing things that middle class people have: If middle class people go to college and own homes, then surely if more people go to college and own homes, we'll have more middle class people. But homeownership and college aren't causes of middle-class status, they're markers for possessing the kinds of traits—self-discipline, the ability to defer gratification, etc.—that let you enter and stay in, the middle class. . . One might as well try to promote basketball skills by distributing expensive sneakers."— Glenn Reynolds, *Washington Examiner*

"When we make (mathematical) models involving human beings we are trying to force the ugly stepsister's foot into Cinderella's pretty glass slipper. It doesn't fit without cutting out some of the essential parts."—Emanuel Derman, from his book, *Models Behaving Badly*.

"You are kidding yourself if you think you can be one of the highest taxed states in the union, have a reputation for being antibusiness—and have a rosy economic future."—Candidate for New York governor Andrew Cuomo, prior to the 2010 fall election. A year later, as governor, he announced agreement with proposed legislation to raise taxes on higher paid individuals making it likely that individuals and businesses will leave the state in droves, resulting in less overall tax receipts for the state. When will they ever learn?

"If you are not prepared to use force to defend civilization, then be prepared to accept barbarism."—Thomas Sowell

"Red meat and gin."—Julia Child, known for her many books on French cooking and her TV cooking show, when asked, more than once, what contributed to her longevity. She lived to be 91.

"Rise early. Work hard. Strike oil"—J. Paul Getty, when asked the keys to success.

"The greatest of all Army teams—STOP—We have stopped the war to celebrate your magnificent success."—Telegram sent by General Douglas MacArthur in the Pacific to the coach of the Army football team, which had just defeated Navy 23-7 in their December 2, 1944 matchup, a game heard around the world by the armed forces of the United States on shortwave sets. From *A Team For America: The Army-Navy Game That Rallied A Nation* by Randy Roberts.

"Be not inhospitable to strangers—Lest they be angels in disguise."—Yeats

"Who the hell wants to hear actors talk?"—Harry Warner, President of Warner Brothers Studios, 1927

"I feel like I'm living next door to the Simpsons."—Indiana Governor Mitch Daniels, commenting on the action of the Illinois legislature and Governor Pat Quinn to raise the state income tax 67% and another increase in the corporate tax followed by an subsequent attempts to exempt many of the state's businesses from the tax so they wouldn't leave the state. More than a dozen companies have already initiated plans to leave Illinois for Indiana.

"Once his book proofs had been approved for press, (Honore de) Balzac would head to a restaurant to celebrate. In one sitting, he was said to have put away a hundred oysters, four bottles of white wine, a dozen salt-meadow lamb cutlets, duckling with turnips, a brace of roast partridge, a Normandy sole, dessert and Comice pears. Afterward, he would send the bill to his publishers."—Anka Muhlstein, from her book *Balzac's Omelette*

"Oh, wow. Oh, wow. Oh, wow."—dying words of Steve Jobs, founder of Apple. One has to wonder what he experienced at that time.

"I am fond of pigs. Dogs look up to us. Cats look down on us. Pigs treat us as equal."—Winston Churchill

"The right to pursue happiness has been perverted into a government-backed entitlement to happiness."—John Stossel

"In passing, also, I would like to say that the first time Adam had a chance, he laid the blame on a woman."—Lady Astor

"It's the good girls that keep the diaries; the bad girls never have time."—Tallulah Bankhead

"Achievement seems to be connected with action. Successful men and women keep moving. They make mistakes, but they don't quit."—Conrad Hilton

"Why doesn't the fellow who says. 'I'm no speechmaker.' let it go at that instead of giving a demonstration?"—Kin Hubbard

"He may be a son-of-a-bitch, but he's our son-of-a-bitch."—President Franklin D. Roosevelt, describing President Somoza of Nicaragua.

"There are three things that can happen when you throw a football and two of them ain't good."—Mike Ditka, replying to sports reporters as to why his offensive game plan didn't include more passes.

"When your argument is weak, pound the table."—Unknown

"There is no educational value in the second kick of a mule."—Unknown

"If you consult enough experts you can confirm any opinion."—Hiram's Law

"I can remember way back when a liberal was one who was generous with his own money."—Will Rogers

"Any new venture goes through the following stages: enthusiasm, complication, disillusionment, search for the guilty, punishment of the innocent, and decoration of those who did nothing."—Unknown

"The suckers haven't permanently deserted the stock market. They are merely waiting until the prices get too high again."—Unknown

"Give me chastity and continence, but not yet."—St. Augustine, a lustful youth at the time, concerned that his prayer might be answered too quickly.

"The environmentalists are for any energy source unless it actually works."—Stephen Hayward, American Enterprise Institute

"If you can't get if from the horse's mouth, you can always find a horse's ass."—Newspaper editor's warning to new reporters.

"Facts are stubborn, but statistics are more pliable."—Mark Twain

"I had a better year than him."—Baseball slugger Babe Ruth's response to reporters when they pointed out to him that under his new contract he was making more money than the President of the United States.

"I think there is a world market for maybe five computers."—Thomas Watson, IBM Chairman, 1943.

"If you like laws and sausage, you should never watch either being made."—Otto von Bismarck

"Abstract Art: A product of the untalented, sold by the unprincipled to the utterly bewildered."—Albert Camus

"A diplomat is a person who can tell you to go to hell in such a way that you actually look forward to the trip."—Caskie Stinnet

"If you're not at the table, you're on the menu."—Unknown. A common belief in Washington regarding participation by lobbyists and company executives in Congressional advisory committees.

"Your manuscript is both good and original; but the part that is good is not original, and the part that is original is not good."—Samuel Johnson

"Stop me before I kill again."—Sign hanging from a tree at a campaign stop of Ronald Reagan, after he stated, "Trees cause more pollution than automobiles do."

"I want there to be one man who will regret my death."—Heinrich Heine, bequeathing his entire estate to his wife, on the condition that she marry again.

"If I have any belief about immortality, it is that certain dogs I know will go to Heaven, and very, very few persons."—James Thurber

"Do you know how to regulate barbers? You don't go back."—Arizona State Senate President Russell Pearce, decrying the burdensome regulations on the state's businesses, including barbers.

"After you've heard two eye-witness accounts of an auto accident, you begin to worry about history."—Unknown

"I'll be glad when this election is over and we can go back to commercials for medicines that have lists of side effects that sound worse than the disease."—Clay Thompson, *Arizona Republic*

"Appeasers believe that if you keep on throwing steaks to a tiger, the tiger will turn vegetarian."—Heywood Braun

"Conscience is the inner voice that warns us that somebody may be looking."—Henry Mencken

"If you tell the truth, have a foot in the stirrup."—Turkish Proverb

"When I hear somebody sigh that 'life is hard,' I am always tempted to ask, 'Compared to what?'—Sydney J. Harris

"The big difference between sex for money and sex for free is that sex for money usually costs a lot less."—Brendan Behan

"The probability of anything happening is in inverse ratio to its desirability."—Gumperson's Law

"We probably wouldn't worry what people think of us if we would know how seldom they do."—Olin Miller

"If all else fails, immortality can always be assured by spectacular error."—John Kenneth Galbraith. The decision of General Custer to attack the Sioux encampment on the Little Big Horn comes immediately to mind.

"Cab drivers are living proof that practice does not make perfect."—Howard Ogden

"The human brain starts working the moment you are born and never stops until you stand up to speak in public."—George Jessel

"Life is like a dog-sled team. If you ain't the lead dog, the scenery never changes."—Lewis Grizzard

"I have never killed a man, but I have read many obituaries with great pleasure."—Clarence Darrow

"Washington is a city of southern efficiency and northern charm."—President John F. Kennedy

"O God, give us serenity to accept what cannot be changed, courage to change what should be changed, and wisdom to distinguish the one from the other."— Reinhard Niebur (The Serenity Prayer)

"When the going gets tough, the tough get going."—Unknown. Motto seen printed, in large letters, on the barracks wall of the Heavy Weapons Platoon of Company B, 1st Airborne Battle Group, 503rd Infantry, 82nd Airborne Division, Fort Bragg, North Carolina, in February 1959.

"The buck stops here."—Famous sign on President Harry Truman's desk

"Moderation in everything."–Aristotle

"The pessimist sees the difficulty in every opportunity. The optimist sees the opportunity in every difficulty."—Winston Churchill

"Better to go forward with an imperfect plan pursued with vigor at the earliest opportunity, than a perfect plan too late."—General George Patton

"I love the challenge of starting at zero every day and seeing how much I can accomplish."—Martha Stewart

"You can't help getting older but you don't have to get old."—George Burns

"Fortune favors the bold."—Virgil

"Use wisely your power of choice."—Og Mandino

"When I look at the future, it's so bright, it burns my eyes."—Oprah Winfrey

"You ain't learning when you're talking."—President Lyndon Johnson

"We don't receive wisdom; we must discover it for ourselves after a journey that no one can take for us or spare us."—Marcel Proust

"Remember that a man's name is to him the sweetest and most important sound in the language."—Dale Carnegie, author of *How to Win Friends and Influence People*.

"You miss 100% of the shots you don't take."—Wayne Gretzky

"Don't make the mistake of letting yesterday use up too much of today."—Will Rogers

"Keep in mind that the true meaning of an individual is how he treats a person who can do him absolutely no good."—Ann Landers

"If you are looking for a friend who has no faults, you will have no friends."—Hasidic folk saying

"Speak when you are angry and you will make the best speech you will ever regret."—Ambrose Bierce

"Expect trouble as an inevitable part of life and repeat to yourself the most comforting words of all: This, too, shall pass."—Ann Landers

"I have missed more than 9000 shots in my career. I have lost almost 300 games. On 26 occasions I have been entrusted to take the game's winning shot...and missed. And I have failed over and over and over again in my life. And that is why...I succeed."—Michael Jordan

"When we hate our enemies, we are giving them power over us—power over our sleep, our appetite, our blood pressure, our health and our happiness. Our enemies would dance with joy if only they knew how they were worrying us, lacerating us and getting even with us. Our hate is not hurting them at all, but our hate is turning our days and nights into a hellish turmoil."—Dale Carnegie

"I didn't waste time."—Bill Gates, Microsoft founder, in response to a question as to the most important factor leading to his success.

"Be the change you wish to see in the world."—Mahatma Gandhi

"A liar needs a good memory."—Quintilian

"Continuous effort, not strength or intelligence, is the key to unlocking your potential."—Winston Churchill

"Individual commitment to a group effort—that is what makes a team work, a company work, a civilization work."—Coach Vince Lombardi

"Enjoy the little things in life, for one day you may look back and realize they were the big things."—Unknown

"The only thing necessary for the triumph of evil is for good men to do nothing."—Edmund Burke

"When I first open my eyes upon the morning meadows and look out upon the beautiful world, I thank God I am alive."—Ralph Waldo Emerson

"The best way to predict your future is to create it."—Peter Drucker

"You can tell more about a person by what he says about others than you can by what others say about him."—Leo Aikman

"Great moments are born from great opportunities."—Herb Brooks, coach of the 1980 U. S. Olympic hockey team

"I think the key with any past is that you recognize and hold onto what you loved and what you gained and you don't attach yourself to what you've lost."—Demi Moore, on how she maintains a friendly relationship with ex-husband Bruce Willis

"Promise only what you can deliver. Then deliver more than you promise."—Unknown

"When I stand before God at the end of my life, I would hope that I would not have a single bit of talent left, and could say, 'I used everything you gave me'."—Erma Bombeck

"A small sample of the oxygen molecules from any breath that anybody took within the past thousand years is certain to be in the next breath you take. Name a historical figure—Lincoln, John Wilkes Booth, Cleopatra, Hitler, your great grandmother. Tiny samples of them all are in the air you have just drawn in."—David Bodanis, author of *The Secret House: The Extraordinary Science of an Ordinary Day*, whose studies indicated that oxygen molecules are in constant motion and can travel up to 1,000 miles in as little as two weeks.

"What counts is not necessarily the size of the dog in the fight. It's the size of the fight in the dog."—Mark Twain

"At peace and sailing into the sunset."—From an obituary notice.